MW00718431

A Gentle Zephyr—
A Mighty Wind:
silhouettes of life
in the Spirit

J. Gerald Harris

Foreword By
Dr. Jerry Vines

Free Church Press
Carrollton, Georgia

ISBN 978-0-9826561-0-5

Printed in the United States of America by
Lightning Source, Inc.

Cover Design by Jessica Anglea, www.jessicaanglea.com

Unless otherwise indicated, all Scripture taken from the King James Version of the Holy Bible

Free Church Press
P.O. Box 1075
Carrollton, GA 30112

Foreword

The Person and the Work of the Holy Spirit is a neglected area of Christian theology. It is also a source of much incorrect theology. Doctrinal error and excess have caused some to avoid the subject altogether. The result is a loss of power and effectiveness in the lives of individual Christians in particular and the church in general.

This makes the excellent presentation of Dr. Gerald Harris all the more helpful. Dr. Harris is one of our finest writers and teachers of the Word of God. Multitudes are blessed by his articles in The Christian Index. They will now be blessed by this scholarly, yet practical book on the Holy Spirit.

Dr. Harris takes a new and fresh approach to the whole subject of the Spirit's Person and work. He takes us to the Old Testament and New Testament words for the Spirit and reminds us that the same words are used for "breath." In excellent exegesis He takes us from the Spirit's breath in creation to the solemn fires of destruction.

Dr. Harris is scholarly, but also very down to earth. You will profit from his word studies, and will be blessed by his practical applications. He uses personal illustration to help make the profound simple.

I am delighted Dr. Harris has labored to give us this work. You will be blessed as you read it. I pray the breath of the Spirit may blow upon our lives and our churches in a fresh and powerful way as we read and study this volume.

Jerry Vines,
Pastor Emeritus,
First Baptist Church, Jacksonville, Florida;
Two time President,
Southern Baptist Convention;
President, Jerry Vines Ministries, Inc.

Acknowledgments

I t would be extremely rare for a book to be published without a cadre of people providing assistance and fanning the flame of creativity. The finished product you hold in your hand is no exception. First, I am grateful to my selfless wife, who allows me to spend the nights I have at home writing even though my days are spent at the office or on the road.

I am grateful to my boss and Georgia Baptist Convention Executive Director, Dr. J. Robert White, who encourages our staff to write and stretch our faith.

I am indebted to members of my staff, Joe Westbury, Heidi Hager and Donna Ward, who have gone the second mile by helping prepare and proof the final copy of *A Gentle Zephyr – A Mighty Wind.*

Jerry Vines, who has put his reputation on the line by writing the foreword to this book, is not only a great man of God, but also a powerful preacher and a prolific writer. Through the years his sermons have not only blessed my life, but also served as an example of homiletical genius to thousands of preachers, me included. I am eternally grateful for the generous words in his foreword.

Kudos must also be offered to the kind gentlemen who dared to endorse this book in writing. Their names are household words in American Christianity and their grace is certainly evidenced in their willingness to commend this book.

Table of Contents

Foreword by Dr. Jerry Vines 3

Introduction 9

Chapter 1 Creation by Divine Decree 11

Chapter 2 Divine Respiration 27

Chapter 3 The Power to Asphyxiate 45

Chapter 4 The Breath that Births 61

Chapter 5 Holy Exhalation 85

Chapter 6 Theopneustos – The God-Breathed Word .. 105

Chapter 7 A Boneyard + A Breath = A Battalion 123

Chapter 8 A Rushing, Mighty Wind 143

Chapter 9 The Torment of Tophet 163

Author's Notes 181

This book is dedicated to the most superlative "grand-mommy" I know, my wife, Martha Jean, and to ten incomparable grandchildren who have given validity to the old adage: "Grandchildren will fill a space in your heart that you never knew was empty." The terrific ten are: Hayley, Harris and Hope Godwin and Grace, Luke, Mark, Hudson, Brinley, Alden and Maleah Harris

Introduction

I have always been fascinated by the wind. Several years ago my wife, Martha Jean, and I were at Panama City Beach when people were vacating the area by the droves. A tropical storm that had hurricane potential was headed up Florida's west coast and headed toward the Florida panhandle. I knew we had to leave the area, but I really wanted to stay. I have always wanted to ride out a hurricane. I think being a storm chaser would be a thrilling occupation. Those fantasies may not be founded in great wisdom, but the force of the wind has always intrigued me.

Both the Hebrew word, "ruach" and the Greek word, "pneuma" can be translated "wind," "breath" and "spirit." When applied to God, the word "ruach" indicates creative activity (Gen. 1:2) and active power (Is. 40:13). The "ruach" has no boundaries and no recognized destination. Among the Hebrews the "ruach" or wind of God was said to have brooded over the chaos in the story of creation in order to bring forth life.

The wind was also assumed by the Jewish mind to have come from God. "Thou didst blow with thy wind," proclaims the book of Exodus 15:10, and "There went forth a wind from the Lord," declares the book of Numbers 11:31. God might have been defined by these ancient people as a distant, theistic, personal power who lived beyond the sky, but in the wind which they felt on their own faces, they began to sense God as a personal, ever present reality.

The "pneuma" or spirit is never seen. All that is ever seen is what the spirit, wind or breath causes, motivates, inspires, encourages, illuminates, stimulates, provokes, stirs, influences, or activates.

In these messages we will explore the dynamics of the Old Testament "ruach" and the New Testament "pnuema." From the breath of God that brings the world into existence to the breath of God that fuels the fires of Tophet we shall see the power of the Spirit of God – sometimes expressed in a gentle zephyr and sometimes manifested in a mighty wind.

"The Uncreated Spirit smiled and then He laughed out loud. He laughed with shining, moist eyes. His laughter rose like a waterfall of joy. The Uncreated Creator opened His mouth. He parted his lips. He unleashed the mighty primal shout. His words poured out from within. They advanced into the waiting silence like a mighty consuming fire. This was the ancient command that shook into existence the universe." [1]

—*Paul Richardson*

Creation By Divine Decree
Psalm 33:5-9

The words "breathe" and "speak" are often used synonymously. For example, someone might well say, "This matter is confidential! Don't breathe a word of it!" In this case the word "breathe" is used for the word "speak."

Moses, in giving his Genesis account of creation, indicates that God spoke the universe into existence. For example, on the second day of creation the record states, "And God said, Let there be firmament...and God called the firmament heaven..." (Gen. 1:6,8). The Psalmist gives his inspired account of creation by writing, "By the word of the Lord were the heavens made; and all the host of them by the breath of his mouth" (Ps. 33:6).

The design and creation of the universe, as expansive and magnificent as it is, presented no problem for our omnipotent and omniscient God. The heavens with the galaxies, the stars, the moons, and the planets, the earth with its rivers and rills, its mountains and hills, are all a product of His divine decree. He breathed all of it into existence.

I remember my first conscious effort to bring something into existence. I was a fourth grader in Vacation Bible School. All the boys were given six pre-cut pieces of wood and perfectly clear instructions on how to build a "shoe shine" box. These Vacation Bible School creations were to be given to our dads on Father's Day. Every shoebox looked as if it had come off an assembly line except for mine. My dad thought his shoebox was a feeder for the chicken coop.

I should have taken "Industrial Arts" as one of my electives in high school. I didn't! Consequently, I am a mechanical klutz. Several years later my attempt to rectify a slight plumbing problem resulted in a minor flood and major ridicule from the family. When one of the elements in our oven burned out one year, the family members launched a united, concerted effort to discourage my involvement in the simple replacement of the element. You have never seen such solidarity as they vehemently protested my effort to solve the problem.

You can well imagine my frustration and near depression the year Christmas Day almost dawned before I had managed to assemble two bicycles for our twin sons. When the all-night project was completed, I had managed to assemble two vehicles that were reasonable facsimiles of bicycles. I must admit that I was somewhat bewildered by the unusual number of spare parts that remained when the project had been completed.

I have always had difficulty making something out of manufactured parts, even with the aid of explicit instructions. Therefore, you can understand my appreciation and adoration for our divine Creator who made out of nothing an intricate, complex, indescribably beautiful universe with the breath of his mouth.

Genesis 1:1 declares, "In the beginning God created the heavens and the earth." The Hebrew word used in the text for create is "bara." This Hebrew word refers to the origin of something new, rare, and wonderful. It suggests the production of something of inestimable worth, which only God could bring into existence. It means that the material, tangible things of this cosmos are not self-produced. This word "bara" refutes the concept of evolution and affirms the truth of absolute creation. God breathed a divine utterance and this world came into existence. There is a Latin phrase, "creatio ex nihilo," which means "created out of nothing." That is precisely what God did when He breathed this cosmos into existence. He stepped out into space and took nothing heaped upon nothing and nothing compressed upon every side with nothing and nothing undergirded by nothing and made the universe.

The amazing thing is that men sweat and toil, exhaust their energies, tax their mental capacities, and strain every fiber of their being in order to construct some "tower of Babel" out of already existing material. But, God had only to utter a word and create the star spangled heavens, this beautiful, bountiful earth, and the inhabitants thereof.

The Goodness Of God In Creation

The Psalmist declares, "...the earth is full of the goodness of the Lord" (Ps. 33:5b). The Bible also avows that the earth is full of

God's mercy (Ps. 119:64), full of God's riches (Ps. 104:24), and full of God's glory (Is. 6:3). The handiwork of God, the cosmos that He has created, reveals His character. Indeed, the Bible portrays our great God throughout its pages as a God of goodness.

There was a day when Moses wanted desperately to enter into God's presence and see God's glory. He prayed that he might see a visible, profound, confluent expression of deity. However, God said, "Thou canst not see my face: for there shall no man see me, and live" (Ex. 33:20). Nevertheless, God made a concession to Moses and said, "...I will make all my goodness pass before thee, and I will proclaim the name of the Lord before thee: and will be gracious to whom I will be gracious, and will show mercy on whom I will show mercy" (Ex. 33:19).

In reality God is a spirit and as such is invisible to mankind, but He has expressed Himself to us in a myriad of ways. He has revealed Himself by His many names and titles, by His incomparable attributes, and by the written Word. Of course, the ultimate and most comprehensive revelation of God was embodied in His only begotten Son "who is the image of the invisible God...." (Col. 1:15a).

However, we must not fail to see God in creation. His goodness is imprinted upon every field and flower. God could have made everything taste like castor oil. He could have filled the atmosphere with the pungent and offensive odor that emanates from the skunk. He could have made everything we see grotesque, dark, and frightening. He could have made everything that we touch irritating and unpleasant. He could have made every sound comparable to the unnerving noise of fingernails screeching across a chalkboard. On the contrary, God's creation reflects His goodness.

14

The Beauty Of God's Masterpiece

Let us consider some of the ways in which this attribute of God is evident in the beauty of His created masterpiece. The Bible says, "He hath made everything beautiful in his time...." (Eccl. 3:11). For example, think about the visually soothing pale blue of the sky as contrasted with the velvet green carpet of grass with which God has covered the earth. Consider the multi-colored rainbow that appears in the summer sky after a downpour of rain. Furthermore contemplate the stately beauty of the giant sequoias and the intricate design of the delicate orchid both of which speak of the goodness of God in creation.

Quite a few summers ago, on a family trip to the west coast, we drove north of Klamath Falls, Oregon, to Crater Lake National Park. This beautiful park is located in the Cascade Mountain Range. In mid-July we drove to an elevation exceeding 8,000 feet above sea level where snow covered the ground and banks of snow lined the highway. When at last we emerged from the car and walked to the edge of the crater, we saw a spectacular, breath-taking view. A beautiful lake with indigo blue water filled the bottom of the crater. Rising out of the lake was Wizard Island covered with evergreen trees. The pure white snow at ground level, the dark pumice volcanic residue that lines the sides of the crater, the sparkling blue water below graced with this emerald island in the midst of it gave ample evidence of the majesty and goodness of God.

The Utility Of God's Masterpiece

Musing over the goodness of God in creation, we are reminded not only of the beauty of God's creative masterpiece, but also of the utility of His created masterpiece. Everything, which God has made, has a distinct purpose, and the universe is simply a storehouse of divine provision of all of life's necessities.

Do you remember the means whereby God brought this world into existence? The universe was created by divine decree. On the third day of creation God breathed all plant life into being. Interestingly, all plant life breathes. It is through a process of photosynthesis and respiration that all vegetation is sustained.

Animals likewise breathe and, as they do, carbon dioxide passes out of the lungs in respiration and is absorbed by plants. In the plants the carbon dioxide goes through a process known as glycolysis, whereby food is constructed for the plant. The vegetation then releases oxygen, which is absorbed by the lungs of animals. Herein we have one distinct way in which plants and animals are useful to one another. The animals have a purpose in that they supply carbon dioxide for the plants; the plants have a purpose in that they provide oxygen for the animals. God's creation is not only a thing of beauty; but it is also a thing of utility.

Moving from generalizations to specifics, let us isolate one plant and think of it specifically. Consider the peanut: a rather humble, insignificant, leguminous, annual herb, yet it is an extremely useful creation. George Washington Carver, the famed scientist of Tuskegee Institute, got on his knees before God and, admitting his limited brain power, asked God to teach him everything that there was to know about the peanut. God answered the prayer of Mr. Carver and gave him untold insight concerning this one agricultural product and the ways it could be used for the good of mankind. Consequently, George Washington Carver discovered three hundred products, which can be derived from the peanut. These products include instant coffee, mayonnaise, cheese, chili sauce, shampoo, polish, plastics, and many more. Oh, that God would open our eyes to His broad provision for us found throughout His creation!

The Diversity Of God's Masterpiece

But, as we think about the goodness of God in creation, we are reminded not only of the beauty of it and the utility of it, but we are also reminded of the diversity of His created masterpiece. On this earth God has created deserts and rain forests, Polar Regions and tropical isles, high mountains and deep valleys. The great diversity is a grand display of the wisdom and goodness of God.

This diversity, for example, is seen in the fuel provided in various regions of the world. The industrialized nations of the world take uranium from the earth and translate it into fuel at nuclear power plants. In many places coal and oil are also used for fuel and energy. In other areas the trees of the forest furnish wood, which is a perpetually renewed supply of fuel for many homes. Where sufficient supplies of wood are not available, the mountaineer may be seen on the lofty highlands gathering peat or turf to warm his cottage through the cold winter months. The Eskimo or the Laplander will kill a whale or a walrus and use the blubber of these marine mammals for fuel. The diversities seen in the provision of fuel for the various regions of the earth are an evidence of the goodness of God in creation.

The Greatness Of God In Creation

Having seen the goodness of God in creation in our text, the Psalms reminds us of the greatness of God when it declares, "By the word of the Lord were the heavens made; and all the host of them by the breath of his mouth" (Ps.33:6). By a mere utterance, God's holy breath, the heavens and earth were created. Genesis 1:3 declares, "And God said, let there be light: and there was light." A more literal rendering of the original text might well be, "And God said, 'Light be, and light was.'" His words are authoritative and when He speaks it is done. God isn't just good; He's great -- great in power and authority over all creation.

When God created this universe He did not have to form a committee. He did not have to secure an architectural firm or a general contractor. Neither did He have to enlist the service of a fundraiser. He did not have to go into the work force and look for laborers. Had all those men and services been available, they would have been unnecessary to the God who can create a world with a word, the cosmos with a command, the planet with a pronouncement, the universe with an utterance.

By a word, a divine exhalation, a breath, the worlds were created and are likewise sustained. Peter says that the universe was created "by the word of God" and that "the heavens and the earth, which are now, by the same word, are kept in store, reserved unto fire against the Day of Judgment...." (2 Ptr. 3:5,7). In Hebrews we are instructed that even now the Lord is "upholding all things by the word of his power" (Heb.1:3). What we have here is instantaneous creation and continuous preservation. The theories of theistic evolution and progressive creation are both eliminated by this "creation by divine decree." In fact, all that God has created will continue until he draws the final curtain and decides to "make all things new" (Rev. 21:5)

What a testimony to God's greatness, that when He brought this world into existence He didn't have to turn one finger to do so! All He had to do was speak. The Word of God is powerful, omnipotent. His promises are sure and His commands stand fast. He can do more with a word, a breath, in an instant than all the combined powers of this earth can do in an eternity.

As we shall see in these messages, the breath of God is an awesome thing. The Hebrew word for breath is "ruach." In fact, the last three letters are pronounced as a faint breath. This Hebrew word, which is little more than an exhalation, is the name used throughout the Old Testament for the Holy Spirit.

In Genesis 17, God changed Abram's name to Abraham and Sarai's name to Sarah. Donald Grey Barnhouse explains, "He added a breath to both names as a symbol of the fact that He was now putting His Holy Spirit within them for a special work. At the end of their century of living by natural means, they came to the beginning of living by supernatural means. God henceforth breathed through them. The names were now Abrah-a-a-m and Sara-a-a-h."[2] Barnhouse's thought is that God breathed through Abraham and Sarah and the supernatural result was the birth of Isaac, the son of promise. "God breathed and life-less Abram became life-full Abraham. God breathed and life-less Sarai became life-full Sarah."[3]

It is incredible that the breath of God can quicken an impotent 99-year-old Abraham and make productive a 90-year-old Sarah who had been barren all her life. It is obvious in the Word of God that the breath of God can create, enliven, restore, empower, and even consume. The power of God manifested by His breath attests to His greatness.

The Genius Of God In Creation

God's creative genius is portrayed in verse 7 of our text in which the Psalmist declares, "He gathereth the water of the seas together as a heap: he layeth up the depth in storehouses." Scholars are divided as to the meaning of this verse. There are two prevailing opinions. One view pertains to the creative genius of God manifested on the third day of creation when He said, "Let the waters under the heaven be gathered together unto one place...and the gathering together of the waters called he seas...." (Gen. 1:9-10).

Prior to the third day of creation, the waters covered the entire surface of the earth. On that third day, however, large tracts of land emerged from the water as vast hollows were carved out for the seas and oceans. With scarcely a whisper God brought forth the land for habitation and channeled the waters into the huge cavities of the earth.

The second view of verse 7, suggests that this "gathering of the waters into a heap" is a reference to the experience recorded in Exodus 15:8, and Joshua 3:13-16. In Exodus 14 the children of

Israel were at the shore of the Red Sea with the surf rushing in toward their feet. The Egyptian army was in hot pursuit and for the children of Israel to turn back into their hostile hands would have been unadvisable, even disastrous. Moses said to the people, "Fear ye not, stand still, and see the salvation of the Lord, which he will show to you today...." (Ex. 14:13).

The Bible declares, "And Moses stretched out his hand over the sea; and the Lord caused the sea to go back by a strong east wind all that night, and made the sea dry land, and the waters were divided. And the children of Israel went into the midst of the sea upon the dry ground: and the waters were a wall unto them on their right hand, and on their left" (Ex.14:21-22).

When Moses and the children of Israel decided to express this experience in their hymn of praise to God, they sang, "And with a blast of thy nostrils the waters were gathered together, the flood stood upright as a heap, and the depths were concealed in the heart of the sea" (Ex.15:8). The phrase, "the blast of thy nostrils," once again speaks of the omnipotence of God's breath.

The passage in Joshua 3 is similar because it records the miracle God wrought when the waters of the Jordan River were divided at flood time to make a dry passageway for the Israelites to enter the land of Canaan. It is expressive of the genius and majesty of God, however, that He could accomplish these miracles with the breath of His mouth, the blast of His nostrils.

Man has mustered all of his architectural and engineering skills and constructed passageways over and through the seas. Think of the brain trust, the manpower, the time, the energy, and the resources necessary to construct the Chesapeake Bay Bridge and tunnel. The planning for this project began in 1956, and the bridge-tunnel was opened for traffic eight years later. Most of this highway has been constructed over the Chesapeake Bay, but there are two concrete-lined tunnels that are each a mile long carrying the roadway deep beneath the main channel of the bay. This was a project that cost millions of dollars. It was a hazardous engineering feat. The underwater tunneling was difficult. The forced draft ventilation system to provide fresh air in the tunnels was a complex and costly process. That which exhausts man physically and pushes him to the limits of his mental power is not even a challenge to an omnipotent God. God had absolutely no trouble making a passageway through the Red sea and through the Jordan River for the children of Israel. With the breath of His mouth, it was all accomplished.

Moreover, the water and the elements He created are subject to His command. The writer of Job said, "For he saith to the snow, Be thou on the earth; likewise to the small rain, and to the great rain of his strength. . .by the breath of God frost is given: and the breadth of waters is straightened" (Job 37:6, 10).

It is interesting that modern technology has brought us to the time when men are trying to control the weather. In 1946, after much study, two American meteorologists attempted to produce artificial rain by a process, which has come to be known as "cloud seeding." By flying in a light aircraft, scientists now use silver iodide, or dry ice, to induce the water vapor in certain clouds to condense as raindrops. The effectiveness of this technique in controlling the weather is questionable.

A good example occurred during the Viet Nam war. The United States military intelligence wanted to impede the movements of the Viet Cong. Someone had the brilliant idea that a torrential rain would immobilize the Viet Cong. The United States Air Force dropped 47,000 pounds of silver iodide over the country in an attempt to produce rain. It did rain and unbelievably so, but the meteorologists said that it would have rained anyway. It seems that the American military brain trust ordered the silver iodide to be dropped just before the monsoon season.

Another example of man's feeble attempts to duplicate weather is evident at winter resorts where snow skiing is popular. All of these places need snow in order to survive, and the demand for snow has prompted modern technology to develop snowmaking machines. Engineering corporations have emerged on the scene to design and install the automatic snowmaking systems, which are used to provide the artificial snow. These systems consist of water and air hydrants, air compressors, pumps, and snow guns. These systems are expensive, environmentally unattractive, and are still dependent upon freezing temperatures in order to be effective. Even then, their quality of snow is inferior to the real thing. Only God is able to make the "real thing". He creates snow flakes by the billions and makes all of them hexagonal; each one is unique – a testimony of the genius of God.

It is by divine decree that God sends rain upon the earth (Job 28:26). Concerning the snow, Job 37: 6, declares, "For he saith to the snow, be thou on the earth . . .". In Job 37: 10, the Word of God says "By the breath of God frost is given…". Then the Bible tells us that when God wants to melt the snow, the ice, and the frost. He does it with the Word of His mouth (Ps.147:16-18). That which men struggle to do in their frailty, God does to perfection in His omniscience. Thus, we see the genius of God in creation.

The Goal Of God In Creation

The goal of God in creation is to draw mankind's attention to the fact that there is a divine creator who is to be reverenced and worshiped. In verse 1 of Psalm 33, the righteous alone are specified as having a right to "praise" the Lord. However, in verse 8, "all the earth" is called upon to "fear" the Lord and hold Him in "awe." As the inhabitants of the earth consider the goodness, the greatness, and the genius of God in creation, surely there is sufficient motivation to bow before the creator of this universe in reverence and awe. To call us past the creation to the Creator is certainly the goal of God in creation.

In Psalm 19:1, God's Word says, "The heavens declare the glory of God; and the firmament showeth his handiwork." Acts 14:17 declares that God "left not himself without witness, in that he did good, and gave us rain from heaven, and fruitful seasons, filling our hearts with food and gladness." In addition to all creation bearing witness to God's greatness, the Lord Himself has given unto man the ability to intuitively know Him (see Rom.1:19).

Often the question is asked, "What about those who have never heard the Gospel? Will they be saved?" In addition to that intuitive knowledge about God, creation itself manifests the goodness, the greatness, and the genius of the Master Architect of this universe. I fully believe that when a person is sensitive to the miracle of creation and responds correctly to the truth that is available, God will reveal more truth to that person until he ultimately comes to the truth of Christ. To the genuine seeker of truth the knowledge of God, the Creator, will at last lead to the knowledge of God, the Father of the only begotten Son, who is the Savior of the world.

For example, a tall black man with sinewy muscles and piercing eyes stands in the spray of Victoria Falls in the heart of Africa. He admires the beauty of nature around him and says, "There must be a God somewhere." He kneels down, not in praise of this visible spectacle on earth, but in praise of the invisible sovereign in heaven. That man may not have enough truth to be saved, but he is responding rightly to the truth he has. God, therefore, will give to that man more truth. If that man continues to honestly and positively respond to the truth God provides, he will one day come to know Christ as "the way, the truth, and the life " (Jn. 14:6). Furthermore, God will do whatever it takes to provide truth to the genuine seeker of truth. He said, "And ye shall seek me, and find me, when you shall search for me with all your heart" (Jer. 29:13).

While there is a great need to be concerned about the lost aboriginal tribe that has never heard the Gospel, there is also a great need to be concerned about our own response to the truth. We have observed the goodness, the greatness, the genius, and the goal of God in creation. We not only have the testimony of the stars and planets and the beauty of nature, but we also have the testimony of the Word of God and the witness of the Holy Spirit. How are we responding to the amount of truth that we have? Jesus said, "...for unto whomsoever much is given, of him shall much be required...." (Lk. 12:48). Somehow, I have an idea that God is going to hold us accountable not only for what we have seen and heard, but also for what we would have seen and heard had we looked and listened.

The one who breathed this universe into existence and controls the course of every planet and knows the flight of every sparrow certainly deserves our worship and can be trusted to have complete control of our lives.

The book of Jonah provides an example of God's sovereignty over His creation. He controlled the wind (Jon. 1:4), the sea (1:13), the fish of the sea (1:17), the vegetation of the earth (4:6), and even a worm that crawled in the dust (4:7). All that God had created responded to His command. Only man, Jonah, was rebellious toward his creator. The Bible declares that, "...Jonah rose up to flee unto Tarshish from the presence of the Lord...." (Jon. 1:3).

Why must man live in rebellion against his Creator? In Revelation 4 the apostle John unveils a scene in heaven where the corridors of glory are reverberating with praise. "The four and twenty elders fall down before Him that sat on the throne, and worship him that liveth for ever and ever, and cast their crowns before the throne, saying. Thou art worthy, O Lord, to receive glory and honor and power: for thou hast created all things, and for thy pleasure they are and were created" (Rev. 4:10-11). So, if God created all things for His pleasure, surely He gets the most pleasure when we, His creation, worship Him, adore Him, reverence Him, and obey Him.

God created this world by divine decree. "He spoke, and it was done; he commanded, and it stood fast" (Ps.33:9). Those who believe in the theory of evolution are victimized by their own gullibility. Those who believe in the Biblical account of creation are led to worship God and submit to His sovereignty.

So, God literally blew life into everything that lives: everything that is animated. Breath is "ruach." It's the same word as "wind." It is the same word as "spirit." Although He breathed life into all living creatures, only into man is God breathing life that is "in His own image. "There is no evolution here. There is no time here. There is no process. There is no mutating. There is no survival of the fittest. There was no pre-Adamic man of any kind. There is no pre-human man. There is no transitional man. I am constantly amazed and I supposed amused at the bizarre, unfounded, confused machinations of evolution that have created nothing but an inexplicable, irrational, unprovable, chaotic complex of tangled schemes to explain what God said in one verse."
—*John MacArthur* [4]

DIVINE RESPIRATION
Genesis 2:7

On several occasions I have run in the annual July 4th Peachtree Road Race in Atlanta. It is a 10K race that typically starts at Lenox Square Mall and ends 6.2 miles later in Piedmont Park. There is something exhilarating about running in such a highly visible race with 50,000 other people. I have always been amazed at the attire of some of the runners. I have seen folks run in tuxedos, Confederate army uniforms, clown outfits and evening gowns. I never expected to finish near the front of the race with all the lean, athletic Kenyan runners, but I am happy to say that I never finished last either.

One year as I turned off Peachtree Street to jog the last few blocks into Piedmont Park, I saw that one of my fellow runners had fallen to the pavement. Other runners had stopped to offer assistance and one was applying cardiopulmonary resuscitation (CPR). He continued this mouth-to-mouth resuscitation and intermittent chest compression until the paramedics arrived. We later learned that the man's life was spared by the quick response of the runner who was able to administer the CPR.

Some years earlier I witnessed a woman being rescued by a lifeguard at Myrtle Beach, South Carolina. The artificial respiration, which he knowingly provided, undoubtedly saved her life.

The first such account of artificial respiration is recorded in Genesis 2:7, when God breathed into the first man, Adam, the breath of life: "And the Lord God formed man of the dust of the ground, and breathed into his nostrils the breath of life; and man became a living soul" (Gen. 2:7).

I'm reminded of the story of the woman who was strolling down the beach when suddenly she saw a crowd of people gathered in a huddle. Curiosity got the best of her and she elbowed her way through the crowd to the horrifying discovery that her husband was the object of everyone's attention. He was lying lifelessly on his back. The lifeguard was hovering over him administering aid.

"That's my husband!" the woman screamed. "What are you doing to my husband?"

The lifeguard looked up and replied, "What do you think I'm doing? I'm giving him artificial respiration!"

The woman shouted, "Artificial nothing! Give him the real thing!"

We can be sure that when God breathed into the nostrils of Adam, He gave him the real thing. That first man was the recipient of divine respiration. Furthermore, we are told that Adam became "a living soul."

The Marvelous Characteristics Of Jehovah God

In the first chapter of Genesis "Elohim" is the Hebrew word used for God. It is a word that is used over 2,500 times in the Old Testament. Elohim is the name that emphasizes the majesty and the power of God. It is the name that identifies God as the Creator.

However, there are many other names for God. No one name is comprehensive enough to include the extent of His power, the depth of His wisdom, the perfection of His holiness, and the fullness of His grace. No one name could contain everything there is about God.

In the second chapter of Genesis, we are introduced to a new name for God. Instead of "God" (Elohim), it is "the Lord God" (Jehovah Elohim). This new name for God is introduced in verses 4 and 5. It reappears in verse 7 and is prominent throughout the Scriptures. In fact, the term "Jehovah" appears over 6,800 times in the Old Testament.

"Elohim" is the creative name for God. It identified God as awesome and omnipotent. However, it suggests aloofness, a God who is perhaps a vague, far off, impersonal deity.

"Jehovah" is the redemptive name for God. It emphasizes God's covenant relationship with man as Jehovah God reveals Himself in all His essential, moral, and spiritual characteristics.

God's Name Is A Sovereign Name

"Jehovah" actually stems from the verb "to be." He is the eternally existent One. He was, He is, and He will forever be. He is the great "I Am." In Exodus 3, Moses had his burning bush experience. Moses was tending the sheep of his father-in-law, Jethro. He was walking along familiar paths on the backside of a desert in Midian. Suddenly, Moses saw a bush on fire, but not being consumed. It was upon that occasion that Moses was called by the Lord to deliver the children of Israel out of Egypt.

After remonstrating with the Lord, Moses said, "Behold, when I come unto the children of Israel, and shall say unto them, the God of your fathers hath sent me unto you; and they shall say to me. What is his name? What shall I say unto them?" (Ex. 3:13). Consider the Lord's reply to Moses: "And God said unto Moses, I AM THAT I AM: and he said. Thus shalt thou say unto the children of Israel, I AM hath sent me unto you" (Ex. 3:14).

This name is a sovereign name because it is all-inclusive. Jehovah is the great "I AM" for every pain, every problem, and every predicament of life. To those who are diseased, He says, "I am the Lord that healeth thee" (Ex. 15:26). To those who are destitute, He says, "I am Jehovah-Jireh, your Provider" (Gen. 22:14). To those who are distraught, He says, "I am Jehovah-Shalom, your Peace" (Jud. 6:24). To those who are in darkness, He says, "I am your Light" (Ps. 27:1). To those who are disabled, He says, "I am your Strength" (Ps. 46:1). To those who are directionless, He says, "I am Jehovah Rohi, your Shepherd" (Ps. 23:1). To those who are dead spiritually, He says, "I am the Lord thy God, the Holy One of Israel, thy Savior...." (Is. 43:3).

God's Name Is A Strong Name

Our Jehovah is a God of such marvelous characteristics. As the great "I Am" He supplies every need and fills every longing of the heart. The name "Jehovah" is a sovereign name, but it is also a strong name. Furthermore, the Jehovah of the Old Testament is the Christ of the New Testament. Turn to chapter 18 of John's Gospel to find an illustration of the strength of this name.

The silent retreat of Jesus into Gethsemane had been interrupted by marching feet and clanging swords. The Roman soldiers led by the betrayer, Judas, had come to arrest Jesus. Rather than cringing in fear before this hostile detachment of soldiers and so-called religious leaders, Jesus stepped forward and asked, "Whom seek ye?"

They said, "We seek Jesus of Nazareth!"

In John 18:5, we have Jesus' response. He said, "I am He." In most translations the word "He" is italicized, which means that it does not appear in the original manuscripts. It was added later in an effort to make the text more readable. In this case, however, it dilutes the force and meaning of Jesus' response. What He actually said was, "I Am." With these two monosyllables, Jesus completely disarmed His captors.

The apostle John writes, "As soon then as He had said unto them, I am He, they went backward, and fell to the ground" (Jn. 18:6). The "band of men" referred to in verse 3, evidently signifies the tenth part of a legion of Roman soldiers, or about five hundred men. In Matthew 26:47 we are informed that "a great multitude with swords and staves" accompanied Judas to arrest Jesus. However, instead of advancing to apprehend Him, they retreated before His single, "I Am." Jesus indicated that His name was God's name--a name fully sufficient to demonstrate divine power and majesty.

God's Name Is A Saving Name

However, as we think of the marvelous characteristics of Jehovah God, we observe that His name is not only a sovereign name and a strong name, but it is also a saving name. Jeremiah is speaking of Jehovah when he says, "Yea, I have loved thee with an everlasting love: therefore with lovingkindness have I drawn thee" (Jer. 31:3). Isaiah says that Jehovah is "a just God and a Savior" (Is. 45:21). The Psalmist is speaking of the saving name of Jehovah when he writes, "In thy name shall they rejoice all the day: and in thy righteousness shall they be exalted" (Ps. 89:16).

In the sovereign, strong, saving name of Jehovah we see some of the marvelous characteristics of our great God.

The Meticulous Care Of Jehovah God

The Meeting That Was Arranged

The uniqueness of man and his superiority over the rest of creation become evident in the book of Genesis. Meticulous care was obviously given by Jehovah God when the first man was brought into being. This incredible care is evident in the meeting that was arranged for the making of man. Until it came time for man's origination. God simply and forcefully said, "Let there be...." and the creation process progressed according to His word. But now, in order to climactically conclude the whole project with the creation of man, there is deliberation. There is a fascinating council meeting within the Godhead. God, the Father, presided and said, "Let us make man in our image, after our likeness..." (Gen. 1:26).

Apparently, it was not uncommon for the Godhead to meet in a Trinitarian solemn assembly before the foundation of the world. For example, in one of these pre-dawn of creation council meetings, the Holy Trinity determined that the Lamb of God would be slain for the sins of the world.

"Forasmuch as ye know that ye were not redeemed with corruptible things, as silver and gold, from your vain conversation received by tradition from your fathers; but with the precious blood of Christ, as of a lamb without blemish and without spot: who verily was foreordained before the foundation of the world, but was manifest in these last times for you" (1 Pet. 1:18-20).

This is a beautiful illustration of the fact that God always makes a provision before there is ever a need. In the council halls of heaven, the Godhead determined that there would be a Savior before there ever was a sinner.

So, the Biblical record suggests that the Godhead met on the sixth day of creation to make a determination about the fashioning of man. The wisdom of God, the Father, God, the Son, and God, the Holy Spirit, were combined to conceive the design for the crown of creation. God announced that man, the highest and the most complex of all creatures, was going to be formed and given dominion over the rest of creation.

The Method That Was Adopted

So, the meticulous care of the Lord in this final act of creation is evident in the meeting that was arranged for the making of man. This same meticulous care is seen in the method that was adopted for the making of man. Up until this time God had virtually breathed this world into existence with the Word of His mouth. In Genesis 2:7, the Bible declares that, "the Lord God formed man." Since we believe in the verbal plenary inspiration of Holy Scripture, the choice of the word "formed" is significant.

In the first place, this word suggests that man's body was a distinct and separate creation of God. This well chosen word effectively refutes the theory of evolution, which promotes a gradual progression or metamorphosis resulting ultimately in a homo sapien (man). Furthermore, the word "formed" comes from a Hebrew word which means, "to mold." The concept is clearly portrayed in Jeremiah 18, in the parable of the potter. The potter is carefully, meticulously forming a vessel out of clay. In Genesis 2:7, the thought conveyed is that of God being directly involved in the molding and shaping of man's physical frame. The Psalmist exclaimed, "I will praise thee; for I am fearfully and wonderfully made: marvelous are thy works; and that my soul knoweth right well. My substance was not hid from thee, when I was made in secret, and curiously wrought in the lowest parts of the earth" (Ps. 139:14-15). This personal, hands-on, involvement was the method God adopted for the making of man.

The Meticulous Care That Was Applied

Finally, the meticulous care of Jehovah God is evident in the materials that were applied in the making of man. The body of man has been carefully analyzed and has been determined to contain enough phosphorus to make over 2,000 matches, enough lime to whitewash a chicken coop, and enough iron to manufacture a twenty penny nail. There is a sufficient amount of fat in the human body to make three pounds of soap and enough carbon for a 25-pound bag of charcoal. The average man's body also contains some glycerin, calcium, potassium, magnesia, chlorine, and enough sulphur to delouse a dog.

Now, when God proceeded to fashion a man, did He search the four corners of the earth to find all of the ingredients in proper proportion for the project at hand? I think not. If dust were to be used for the making of a man, did God use gold dust or diamond dust? Absolutely not! He simply scooped up a handful of dust from the ground, blessed it with his omnipotence; and all the ingredients immediately coalesced in a mighty transformation to produce the first human being.

We see some of the same properties in this miracle that we see in the miracle Jesus performed in Cana of Galilee when He changed the water into wine. At that wedding feast Jesus rescued an embarrassed host from a dreadful dilemma by taking jars of ordinary, commonplace water and turning it into the most delicious grape beverage anyone ever tasted. Welch's would love to have the recipe. When God made man. He took an ordinary chunk of clay, or perhaps even a wisp of dust, and fashioned a body composed of a multiplicity of ingredients and perfect in every way.

Though the body of man was complete and intricate in every detail, something was missing. There was no animation, no life, no spirit, no personality, and no vitality. All the materials, all the ingredients necessary for life were present but one. This man, fashioned by God's hand, was not breathing. Obviously, without breath there is no life.

God, therefore, added the final ingredient necessary for man's existence and "breathed into his nostrils the breath of life" (Gen. 2:7). The only way to understand the full significance of this act of divine respiration is to recognize the connection between the word for "breath" and God's Spirit. In Greek and Hebrew the words for "spirit" and "breath" are identical. The Hebrew word "ruach" is translated "breath" and "spirit." The Greek word "pneuma" refers to breath and spirit and wind.

Therefore, when God breathed His breath into man's nostrils, not only was physical life imparted to him, but also something of the divine Spirit as well. That first man, Adam, was indeed made in the image and likeness of God. His fellowship and affinity to God were unique and glorious. He rejoiced to walk with God in the Garden of Eden in the cool of the day.

Tragically, the fellowship Adam enjoyed with God was terribly fractured by disobedience and rebellion. Sin sadly distorted the image that God gave to Adam. Only vestiges of the former glory that God had given to Adam remained. Consequently, succeeding generations have not been made in the image of God, but in the image of fallen, depraved, glory-tarnished Adam.

The truth, however, is that Adam, that first man, was a product of the meticulous care of Jehovah God. The materials that were applied to the making of that man were earthly dust and divine breath. We know that after the Lord had created the land and the seas. He observed that "it was good" (Gen. 1:10). Upon viewing the vegetation, which He brought forth on the third day of creation, "God saw that it was good" (Gen. 1:12). The creation of the heavenly bodies on the fourth day, the fowls of the air and the fish of the sea on the fifth day, and the animal life on the earth on the sixth day were observed by God and noted as "good."

However, upon the creation of man, God stepped back and saw His handiwork and concluded that "it was very good" (Gen. 1:31). This was, indeed, the result of His meticulous care.

The Miraculous Creation Of Jehovah God

Even as God is a trinity, so is man. The triunity of man consists of body, soul, and spirit. The apostle Paul referred to this triunity in 1 Thessalonians 5:23, when he wrote: "And the very God of Peace sanctify you holy; and I pray God your whole spirit and soul and body be preserved blameless unto the coming of our Lord Jesus Christ."

A Body That Is Intricate

Now, as we think about this miraculous creation of Jehovah God, let us consider first that it is a body that is intricate. The human body is the most complex machine known to man. Those who have dedicated themselves to the study of human physiology and anatomy have discovered the wisdom of specialization. There are fewer and fewer general practitioners. For example, those who specialize in blood diseases are hematologists. Those who major in treating glandular disorders are endocrinologists. Those who specialize in the treatment of heart diseases are cardiologists. Those who concentrate on the treatment of disorders of the eye are ophthalmologists.

Actually, the human body is so complex and sophisticated that many specialists are narrowing their interests within the confines of their own particular field of medicine. For example, an orthopedist is a specialist in the locomotor structures of the body, especially the joints, the skeleton, the muscles, and the supporting structures such as the ligaments and cartilage. Now, however, there are orthopedists who specialize in just the hand or the foot.

Think about the circulatory system of the body. The adult body contains about eight to ten pints of blood. The heart pumps ten pints of blood through the body every minute of our lives. There are approximately twenty-five trillion red blood cells carrying oxygen in the human body and thirty billion white blood cells designed by God to fight disease. Although the red blood cells have a life cycle of 120 days, many of the white blood cells have a life of only about twelve hours. The blood travels all over the body through about sixty thousand miles of arteries, veins, and capillaries. The capillaries have a total surface area that would cover a soccer field. There are three feet of capillaries in a piece of skin the size of a postage stamp.

When you begin to think about the elements in the blood and the blood types, the functions of the blood, and particularly the functions of white blood cells alone in fighting diseases, the intricacy of it is amazing. The human body is so elaborate and so complicated that most scientists can comprehend no more than a fraction of its constitution and operation.

A Soul That Is Intriguing

However, this miraculous creation of Jehovah God not only consists of a body that is intricate, but it also contains a soul that is intriguing. Our text says that this man "became a living soul." The Hebrew word for "soul" is "nephesh." This Old Testament word refers to the realm of the mind and the self-consciousness, the psychological part of man. The soul is the seat of the intellect, the emotions, and the will. The psychological make-up of man is most intriguing.

As a pastor I often counseled people with emotional or psychological problems. Oftentimes the problems were far too complicated for my limited skills in psychotherapy. Today there are people who are suffering from all kinds of mental and emotional trauma. The thought processes that will take a person to the heights of brilliance in one case and to the border of insanity in another situation are most intriguing.

There are psychotic disorders, mood disorders, anxiety disorders, adjustment disorders, sleep disorders, sexual disorders, and gender identity disorders. There are neuroses and schizophrenia and phobias by the dozen.

Can you imagine how it must have been in the second chapter of Genesis when man, unblemished by sin, had a pure self-consciousness? Psychologically, his life was ideal. In the beginning man's mind was not corrupted by sin. His emotions were undisturbed by worldliness and his will was unaffected by disobedience. In those early days he had the capacity to live a life without the gray ghost of guilt haunting him. His conscience was clear; and his thought processes were impeccable. His body was perfect physically; and his mind was perfect psychologically.

A Spirit That Is Infinite

Please observe, however, that this marvelous creation of Jehovah God consists not only of a body that is intricate and a soul that is intriguing, but it also includes a spirit that is infinite. The spiritual part of man became a reality when God breathed into man the breath of life. The word "breath" ("ruach") also means "spirit." This is the thing that distinguishes man from the animals—the breath of God. By imparting to man His own immortal breath, God gave to this earthen vessel a never dying spirit.

There was a day when God breathed the very nature of Himself into man. Consequently, man has a special relationship to God by virtue of the divine Spirit. It is possible for man to know God, to experience God, and to worship God.

Unfortunately, what we frequently do is put our eyes upon man rather than on God. Remember that the most noble of men have clay feet. They will often bring disappointment and confusion to the person who has highly esteemed them. Only the Lord can be fully trusted.

Isaiah wrote, "Cease ye from man, whose breath is in his nostrils; for wherein is he to be accounted of" (Is. 2:22)? In other words, "Why should you put your faith in feeble man who can hold only one nose full of breath at a time? Put your faith in God whose supply of breath is inexhaustible." Indeed, it is in the Lord God alone that "we live, and move, and have our being" (Acts 17:28). He is the One to whom we must look for physical life and spiritual life.

Because of the life, which Jehovah God has given to us, we have a moral responsibility to honor Him. In Ecclesiastes 12:1, the Bible says, "Remember now thy Creator...." We are to think upon our

Creator. We are to reflect upon the One who has brought us into being. We are to ponder the majesty and the omnipotence of the One who has given us life. In Isaiah 45:9, God's Word issues the solemn warning, "Woe unto him that striveth with his maker." We dare not rebel against our "Maker, Defender, Redeemer, and Friend."

Think of all that God has graciously provided for us. He has provided for temporal needs and eternal needs, for physical needs and spiritual needs.

> "It took a miracle to put the stars in place,
> It took a miracle to hang the world in space;
> But when He saved my soul, cleansed and made me whole,
> It took a miracle of love and grace"

The miracle of creation and the miracle of re-creation require a response. What is our response to all that God has done for us?

During the First World War, the British soldiers were having a difficult time of it. Their line was under assault and being penetrated during the early days of the conflict. One frightful night when morale was low and the troops had been forced to retreat, one of the chaplains concluded that an observance of the Lord's Supper would be a helpful experience for everyone. He determined to administer the Lord's Supper in a YMCA hut.

The building was not large, but over five hundred men of the Black Watch crowded into that hut. Although many stood and watched, most of them partook of the commemorative supper. The sound of battle could be heard in the distance and enemy shells lit up the evening sky. Upon completing the service, they sang the closing hymn, "When I Survey the Wondrous Cross." As they came to the last verse, the saintly chaplain said, "Let us alter the last line. I do not want you to sing, 'Demands my soul,' but, 'Shall have my soul, my life, my all. ' Sing it that way only if you really mean it, only if it expresses the desire of your hearts, only if you want Christ to have your all."

So, they sang it and, as the benediction was about to be pronounced, a voice from the back of the hut could be heard, "Chaplain, may we sing that last verse again? I was not prepared to sing it the last time, but now I would like to be included in singing the altered version."

The chaplain responded, "Yes, yes, we shall sing it again." The same thing happened over and over again until every soldier in that YMCA hut had sung that verse, "Love so amazing, so divine; shall have my soul, my life, my all."

At the conclusion of that service those men were called out and sent back to the battle. By morning very few of those soldiers remained alive.

In view of all that the Lord has done for us, how can we hold anything back from Him? Our God is Jehovah, and His name is a sovereign, a strong, and a saving name. Without Him we are nothing. The breath of God in us is our life and our glory. He is deserving of our supreme allegiance. Are you willing to say to Him:

"Were the whole realm of nature mine,
That were a present far too small, Love so amazing, so divine,
Shall have my soul, my life, my all?"

"Why do we complain about nature? She has acted kindly: life is long if you know how to use it. But one man is gripped by insatiable greed, another by a laborious dedication to useless tasks...Many are occupied by either pursuing other people's money or complaining about their own... Some have no aims at all for their life's course, but death takes them unawares as they yawn languidly — so much so that I cannot doubt the truth of that oracular remark of the greatest of poets: 'It is a small part of life we really live.' ...You are living as if destined to live forever: your own frailty never occurs to you; you don't notice how much time has already passed, but squander it as though you had a full and overflowing supply." [5]
—*Lucius Annaeus Seneca*

The Power To Asphyxiate
Daniel 5:23

Kurt Krug was flying his private plane from his home in Bridgam, Michigan to Venice, Florida. In the course of his fight, his twin engine Piper Aztec lost electrical power over the mountains of North Georgia. For about thirty minutes he flew in heavy, black clouds without radio, radar, or instruments.

At about 6 pm, the wings of Krug's plane clipped some treetops and the plane crashed into Justus Mountain. The fact that the pilot was not instantly killed or burned to death was a major miracle. The terrific impact caused the pilot to black out. Hours later, in the middle of the night, Krug woke up to the realization that he was trapped in the cockpit and immobilized by a broken arm and broken leg.

Krug had already beaten the odds by surviving a terrifying crash in the rugged, remote high country. Others had survived such crashes in isolated areas only to die of exposure or starvation.

Upon awakening, the broken and bleeding pilot was shivering in the cold, wet cockpit. He managed to wrap himself in a fleece seat cover to keep warm. By mid-morning Saturday the fog was still so thick he could not see the treetops. As the hours passed, the pain increased. The fear intensified. The hope faded. Would the shattered cockpit become Kurt Krug's casket after all?

After being trapped for eighteen hours, the 32-year-old pilot was rescued by three backpackers. Amazingly Krug's plane had gone down within forty yards of the Appalachian Trail. Andres Petras, one of the rescuers, said, "A couple of hundred yards either way and we would have never seen him."

There are those who would say, "Well, it just wasn't Kurt Krug's time to die." I wholeheartedly agree. We are alive today because somehow God, in His providence, has willed it to be so. Not only has Jehovah God breathed into man the breath of life, but He also holds the breath of all mankind in His hands. Life's continuation or termination is God's prerogative. He has it within His power to provide respiration or induce asphyxiation.

The word "asphyxiate" means "to kill or make unconscious through want of adequate oxygen, the obstruction of normal breathing." Indeed, God has the power to asphyxiate. Job is speaking of Jehovah God's omnipotence when he declares, "...the hand of the Lord hath wrought this...in whose hand is the soul of every living thing, and the breath of all mankind" (Job 12:9-10). Our lives, our breath, the length of our days are in God's hand. The same God who has the power to give also has the power to take away (see Job 1:21).

In the text before us, Daniel, the prophet of God, paints a fascinating scene out of his experience in ancient Babylon. Belshazzar, Babylon's king, had ordered a momentous celebration for a thousand of his lords. This festive occasion soon degenerated into a drunken orgy. In the midst of the revelry, Belshazzar commanded his servants to bring in the sacred vessels, which had been taken from the temple in Jerusalem. These vessels had been consecrated for temple use and were not to be touched except for divinely prescribed purposes. However, all the guests at the king's party drank wine from the vessels of gold and praised the pagan deities of Babylon.

When the merriment was at its height, and wine was reducing all inhibitions, a phenomenon occurred that brought immediate sobriety and alarm to everyone in the great banquet hall, particularly to the king. The record states: "In the same hour came forth fingers of a man's hand, and wrote over against the candlestick upon the plaster of the wall of the king's palace: and the king saw the part of the hand that wrote. Then the king's countenance was changed, and his thoughts troubled him, so that the joints of his loins were loosed, and his knees smote one against another" (Dan. 5:5-6). In other words, the appearance of the mysterious hand gave Belshazzar the heebie-jeebies.

In the king's search to find someone to interpret the handwriting on the wall, he was introduced to the Hebrew captive, Daniel. Although the strange writing was both puzzling and perplexing to the Babylonians, Daniel interpreted the cryptic script and preached Belshazzar a considerable sermon in the process. Our text constitutes the climactic point of Daniel's denouncement of the king when he says, "And the God in whose hand thy breath is, and whose are all thy ways, hast thou not glorified" (Dan. 5:23).

The Precious Breath Of Belshazzar

Daniel forthrightly tells the king that his breath is in God's hand. The Creator who gives life and breath can just as easily take both life and breath away. There is a sense in which I believe an individual who walks with God is invincible and indestructible until the divine purpose for that individual is fulfilled. However, God is sovereign and our days are in His hands.

Moses was supposed to have been drowned at birth. Pharaoh had ordered the midwives of Egypt to take all of the baby boys born to Hebrew women and cast them into the Nile River. Obviously, it was not God's will for Moses to die in his infancy. Ironically, Pharaoh's daughter discovered the floating bassinet of Moses in the Nile River, had compassion on Moses, and ended up paying his mother to nurse her own child.

God then preserved Moses' life for 120 years, but at that point the Lord purposed that it was time for Moses to die. A physical examination would have concluded that Moses was robust and in the pink of health. The record says that, "...his eye was not dim, nor his natural force abated" (Deut. 34:7). In other words, at 120 years of age he had not yet had to visit an optometrist, and he would have made a good showing in a triathlon. Nevertheless, when Moses was vibrant and strong, God took away his breath and his life.

Absalom was the son of King David. He had been a rebellious son. Though he lived in Jerusalem, there was a time when he went two full years without even seeing his father's face (see 2 Sam. 14:28). Absalom tried to usurp the authority of his father. He led a revolt against his father, the king. God decided that he would no longer tolerate the insolence of Absalom. As a young man this rebellious son rode a mule under the thick branches of an oak tree and caught his long hair in the boughs of the tree. While hanging there the Bible says that Joab, "Took three darts in his hand, and thrust them through the heart of Absalom while he was yet alive in the midst of the oak" (2 Sam.18:14). God determined that it was the time for the curtain to be drawn on the life of this defiant, disobedient son.

Hezekiah was a good king amidst a long list of evil kings. His biography is summed up in 2 Kings 18:5: "He trusted in the Lord God of Israel; so that after him was none like him among all the kings of Judah, nor any that were before him." On a certain day in the fourteenth year of Hezekiah's reign, he became deathly ill. The Bible reports that he was "sick unto death." Isaiah, the prophet, said to Hezekiah, "Set thine house in order; for thou shalt die, and not live" (2 Kings 20:1). The situation was grim. The physicians were out of remedies. The family had been called to the bedside. The local mortician had a gleam in his eye. The obituary notice was ready to go to the newspaper. The children were trying to decide how to invest the inheritance.

When all hope seemed to be gone, the good king turned his face to the wall and prayed. God heard his prayer and the death sentence was lifted. The blush of life returned to his cheeks and God said, "...I will add unto thy days fifteen years" (2 Kings 20:6).

I am reminded of the man who had been in the intensive care unit of the hospital at the point of death for days. One day the doctor came into the waiting room with a smile on his face. Upon seeing the patient's wife, the doctor said, "I have good news for you. Your husband has taken a remarkable turn for the better. He is going to get well and should be out of the hospital in three days."

The wife said, "Oh, doctor! I don't know what to say. I have already sold his clothes to pay for the funeral!"

We must never presume upon what God will do concerning the length of our days; our life and breath are in His hands. The Bible says, "The days of our years are three score and ten" (Ps. 90:10), but God can add to those years or subtract from those years according to His own will.

When the apostle Paul went to Lystra, he was stoned, thrown out of the city, and left for dead. However, the report of his demise was greatly exaggerated. Imagine how shocked the people of Lystra were when Paul returned to their city several days later after a brief preaching mission in Derbe. God was not yet through with Paul, and his days were not about to be completed until God so willed it. Years later, when Paul had fulfilled God's purpose for his life, he said, "For I am now ready to be offered, and the time of my departure is at hand. I have fought a good fight, I have finished my course, I have kept the faith" (2 Tim. 4:6-7). Surely our life and breath are in God's hands.

It is interesting to note that God determined that two men would never die. Enoch was translated to heaven without having to pass through the barrier of physical death. Elijah was transported to heaven in a chariot of fire on a highway that bypassed the grim reaper. Similarly, God shall determine who shall be alive when Christ returns and all who shall taste of death before that long awaited day. The measure of our days and the extent of our breathing are in His hands.

Think about this: Just as God controls the length of our days so did Jesus control the length of His days here on earth. It was by divine providence that Jesus escaped death as an infant. Herod, the king, sent out a decree that all the children in the region of Bethlehem two years old and under be slain. Joseph took Mary and Jesus by night and escaped the massacre by fleeing to Egypt.

Throughout His earthly ministry, when Jesus' life was threatened. He managed to escape, and the Gospel writers avow that His ability to elude death was possible because His hour had not yet come. In John 7:30, the evangelist writes, "Then they sought to take Him: but no man laid hands on Him, because His hour was not yet come."

When Jesus was in the temple, He professed to be "the light of the world" (Jn. 8:12). He also claimed an identity with Jehovah God. These bold pronouncements no doubt infuriated the Jews, but the Scripture declares that "no man laid hands on Him; for His hour was not yet come" (Jn. 8:20). Concerning His life, Jesus said, "No man taketh it from me, but I lay it down myself. I have power to lay it down, and I have power to take it again..." (Jn. 10:18).

However, when Jesus had entered Jerusalem just prior to His cru-cifixion and certain men came seeking him, He said, "The hours is come, that the Son of man should be glorified" (Jn. 12:23). Even when the soldiers came to arrest Jesus, He avowed that He could evade death if He so desired (see Matt. 26:53). Jesus controlled the length of his days. We need to understand that though Jesus could have extended His days on the earth, He willingly submitted to the scourging of evil men and death on a cross so that we might have eternal life.

But, remember, even as the Lord measured out the length of His days on this earth, so does He measure out our days. Our life and breath are in His hands. This is the message that Daniel communicated to Belshazzar. Life is precious. Every breath is a gift from God. He has the power to provide respiration or induce asphyxiation.

Since every breath we draw is in His hands, we need to recognize our utter dependence upon Him. To try to do anything independent of God, without consulting Him first, is foolish, presumptuous, and rebellious. In as much as He is our source of supply, we need to love Him, honor Him, and live for him now and for as long as it pleases Him to grant us breath.

The Perverse Behavior Of Belshazzar

To the king of Babylon, Daniel preached, "...and the God in whose hand thy breath is, and whose are all thy ways, hast thou not glorified" (Dan. 5:23). Notice specifically the phrase, "...and whose are all thy ways...." The perverse behavior of Belshazzar had not escaped God's notice.

God's candid camera is constantly grinding away to record our actions. His celestial compact disc recorder is forever keeping an account of every conversation. There are both advantages and disadvantages to such constant, divine scrutiny.

Sometimes it is comforting and reassuring to know that God is watching over us. There are days of disappointment. Oftentimes disappointment turns to despair. In those days it is such a blessing to know that God sees our trouble and heartache and that He cares.

When the Israelites had suffered under the bondage afflicted upon them by the Egyptian taskmasters, they must have felt forgotten and forsaken by God. However, God was not ignorant of their unenviable predicament. When God called Moses from the burning bush and commissioned him to lead the Hebrews out of Egypt, He said, "I have surely seen the affliction of my people which are in Egypt, and have heard their cry by reason of their taskmasters; for I know their sorrows" (Ex. 3:7). God is never oblivious to the affliction of His people.

When Jesus chose His twelve disciples, He warned them that persecutions would come, but He also assured them of the watch care of the Heavenly Father. Jesus said, "Are not two sparrows sold for a farthing? And one of them shall not fall on the ground without your Father. But the very hairs of your head are all numbered. Fear ye not, therefore, ye are of more value than many sparrows" (Matt.10:29-31).

The Psalmist declared, "O Lord, thou hast searched me, and known me. Thou knowest my downsitting and mine uprising; thou understandest my thought afar off. Thou compassest my path and my lying down, and art acquainted with all my ways. For there is not a word in my tongue, but, lo, O Lord, thou knowest it altogether" (Ps.139:1-4). The truth is that God knows more about everybody than we know about anybody. That fact is that is has its comforting aspects, but it also has some disturbing aspects.

You see, God not only knows about our sorrows. He also knows about our sins. He is not only aware of the despair in our hearts; He is also aware of the deceit in our hearts. He knows not only about our afflictions; He also knows about our addictions. He not only sees our grief; He also sees our greed. He notices not only our prayers and praise, but also our profanity and perversion.

God was certainly aware of Belshazzar's perverse behavior. This Babylonian king was a man about whom history has nothing good to say. He was a tyrant who used his power to gratify his own desires. He saturated his body and soul in sinful pleasures. He had no reverence for holy things. He desecrated the sacred vessels from the temple in Jerusalem. He lived a life of defiance and rebellion against God. He was weighed on God's balance scales and found wanting. Belshazzar was ripe for the judgment of Almighty God.

One of these days those of you who have rejected Christ and spurned the entreaties of the Holy Spirit will stand before the judgment bar of God. The divine balance scale will be brought out. The evidence will be presented. The omniscient God who witnessed your every transgression and saw your every misdeed will begin to make a catalogue of your sins. Even the things done behind closed doors and the intent of your heart will be revealed on that day. Every evil deed, every impure motive, every idle word, every secret sin like militant soldiers will come marching out of the back alleys and the night scenes and the hidden places; they will all be put on display—exhibit number one, exhibit number two, exhibit number three, exhibit number 300, etc. Suddenly, one side of God's balance scale is weighed down with the load of your sins.

If you have not accepted Christ, you will have no advocate. So, the scene will be like this. The Judge says, "Well, what do you have to say for yourself?"

You swallow hard; the perspiration breaks out on your brow. Your face becomes pale. But, like many others, you begin to think of all the good deeds you have done. You think, "Maybe if I can remember enough of my good deeds that will outweigh all of the bad things that I have done, and I'll be acquitted." You begin to recite the noble deeds: "I paid my debts. I worked with the boy scouts. I gave to charity. I provided for my family. I even went to church...." Even as you speak, God is frowning and shaking His head. He interrupts and says, "To me your good deeds are as filthy rags" (see Is. 64:6). At that point God points an accusing finger in your direction and says, "If that's all you've got to say, I declare that you are guilty, lost, hopelessly lost! Your destiny is hell and there will you spend eternity."

You say, "Well, that seems so unfair!" No, it is altogether fair. God has graciously provided a way for our salvation. The only way to tip those balance scales in your favor is to put Christ opposite your sins. The Word of God says that it is "not by works of righteousness which we have done, but according to His mercy He saved us...." (Titus 3:5). When you trust Christ for your salvation. He becomes both your advocate and your Savior in the Day of Judgment. In fact, there is no judgment to those who are in Christ Jesus (see Rom. 8:1).

The Primary Business Of Belshazzar

The primary business of Belshazzar and every human being is to glorify God. The shorter catechism to which many churches ascribe reads: "The chief end of man is to glorify God and to enjoy Him forever."

Jesus said that we should let our light shine to the glory of God (see Matt.5:16). The Lord Jesus has challenged all of us to bear much fruit so that the Father might be glorified (see John 15:8). When Paul wrote the Roman church, he expressed his desire that they "with one mind and one mouth glorify God…" (Rom.15:6). It was also Paul's prayer that the gentiles might "glorify God in your body, and in your spirit, which are God's" (I Cor. 6:20). Peter added in his first epistle, "If any man speak, let him speak as the oracles of God; if any man minister, let him do it as of the ability which God giveth; that God in all things may be glorified through Jesus Christ, to whom be praise and dominion forever and ever. Amen." (1 Pet. 4:11)

The primary purpose for our existence is that we might live in such a way that we glorify God. This specific purpose was the essence of the life of Christ. The whole of His life is summed up in the words of John 17:4, when He prayed to His father, "I have glorified thee on the earth; I have finished the work which thou gavest me to do."

The absolute opposite of God's glorification is found in the summary of Belshazzar's life in our text: "The God in whose hand thy breath is, and whose are all thy ways, thou hast not glorified" (Dan. 5:23). That is a startling synopsis of this man's wickedness. He had failed to fulfill the primary business of his life.

If anyone wanted to expose the seedy side of Belshazzar, it would not have been difficult. An inventory of his sins could have filled all the books in a library, but in the final analysis sin consists not so much in specific acts of wickedness as in a wrong relationship to God. The king of Babylon had failed to develop a relationship with God. He had not glorified the One who had the power to provide respiration or induce asphyxiation.

One dark, foreboding night Dick Hall discovered that his life and breath were in God's hands. Dick, his wife, Rita, and sons, Simon and James, had moved to Jackson, Mississippi, from England in 1987. Dick was a tall, straight, strong, proper Englishman with a resolute countenance, a stately posture, and a powerful handshake that caused many to wince in pain. While in London he was one of seventy-eight men who served in the Queen's company of the Grenadier Guard, an elite unit of soldiers stationed near Buckingham Palace, the Queen and the royal family.

While pastor of the Colonial Heights Baptist Church in Jackson, I had the privilege of welcoming Rita, Simon, and James Hall into our church on their profession of faith in Christ. Though Rita and the Halls' sons were baptized and integrated into the life of our church, Dick, the proud Englishman, refused to publicly acknowledge a relationship to Christ. He attended church frequently, but there was an aloofness and a distance about him despite a definite appealing charm.

Then the heart attack came. No one expected Dick Hall to be the victim of such a debilitating physical trauma. He had been shot at and bombed in his line of duty at Buckingham Palace. Most people thought he was bullet proof. The heart attack occurred in the middle of the night at home. Rita managed to get him in the car and to the emergency room at St. Dominic Hospital, where the heart stopped.

For three and one-half minutes there was no heartbeat. Dick said, "I went away from this earth. Though it was cold and windy in those dark, early morning hours on that fateful morning, three angels escorted me heavenward in beautiful weather that was balmy and windless. We seemed to float onto a wide avenue. At the far end of this avenue, or boulevard, there was a wall that was so high you could not see the top of it. It was so wide the far ends of the wall were out of view. There was an aura that permeated and surrounded the wall."

Dick Hall testified, "I never got as far as the wall. There was a checkpoint that was visible between the wall and me. When I arrived at the checkpoint, someone asked for my name and I responded, 'My name is Dick Hall.' They checked my name against a list in what I determined to be the Book of Life. They looked, but could not find my name. Some person of authority looked at me and said, 'I'm sorry, Mr. Hall, we have no record of your name. You can go no further, but we are going to let you go back to earth. When you get back to earth, there are two things you must do. You must accept Christ as your personal Savior and you must encourage every Christian you meet to live an all out, 100 percent life for Christ'."

After three and one-half minutes without a heartbeat Dick Hall overcame the flat line on the cardiograph and started breathing again. Within hours the once proud Englishman accepted Christ as his Savior. Dick got a second chance.

Don't be like Belshazzar. Live for God! Bring glory to the Lord of heaven. The God who has the power to provide respiration or induce asphyxiation deserves to receive glory from your life and mine. Indeed, that is our primary business from our first breath until our last.

"It is an excellent thing to have an honest heart and a candid mind, but Christ says even to such men, 'Ye must be born again.' It does not matter how good a man may be, or how earnest he may be in seeking to find the truth, he cannot escape from the necessity which applies to the entire human race, 'ye must be born again.'" [6]
—*Charles Haddon Spurgeon*

The Breath That Births
John 3:1-10

In the 1950's a French obstetrician, Fernand Lamaze, developed a method of psychophysical preparation for childbirth. Today the Lamaze technique is the most widely used method of childbirth available. During the course of pregnancy the expectant mother attends classes where she is informed about the physiology of pregnancy and childbirth. With the help of a "coach," generally the husband, the mother-to-be learns the techniques of relaxation, concentration, and breathing.

Prior to the delivery of the child the mother is urged to find a focal point in the room upon which to concentrate. Some expectant mothers bring stuffed animals, pictures of family members, or cherished keepsakes as objects upon which they will focus their attention during the most intense moments of labor. The ability to concentrate upon these objects help to minimize the pain.

The breathing exercises are absolutely crucial to the success of the Lamaze method of natural childbirth. The breathing that begins with a deep, relaxed, measured rhythm continues toward a shallow, accelerated type of breathing as the contractions progress. Those who use the Lamaze method are often able to avoid any anesthesia during delivery.

We are going to direct our attention to the kind of breath that produces a supernatural birth. We're not talking about Lamaze breathing techniques learned by women approaching childbirth. Although physical life is a miracle, the greater miracle is when the quickening breath of the Spirit of God produces a new creature in Christ Jesus.

John reports Jesus as saying, "Except a man be born of water and of the spirit (pneumatos), he cannot enter into the kingdom of God...that which is born of the flesh is flesh and that which is born of the spirit (pneumatos) is spirit (pneuma)...the wind (pneuma) bloweth where it listeth, and thou hearest the sound thereof, but canst not tell whence it cometh, and whether it goeth; so is everyone that is born of the spirit (pneumatos)" (Jn 3:5, 6, 8).

Please remember that the Greek word "pneuma" or "pneumatos" can be translated "wind," "spirit," or "breath." Therefore, when Jesus speaks of being born of the "pneumatos," He is speaking not only of the wind and the spirit but also of the breath that births. In our text we are introduced to Nicodemus who must learn the importance of being born from above by the quickening breath of the Holy Spirit.

The Advantage Of The New Birth

In the first two verses of our text, the apostle John introduces to us one of the fascinating Jewish leaders of the first century Nicodemus. The apostle declares, "There was a man of the Pharisees named Nicodemus, a ruler of the Jews: the same came to Jesus by night."

Many speculations have surfaced concerning the nighttime visit of Nicodemus. Some scholars have suggested that Nicodemus came to Jesus by night to avoid publicity, that he did not want to have to face the questions and the harassment of his colleagues. Others have concluded that Nicodemus did not want a public encounter to enhance the rising popularity of the young rabbi from Nazareth. Still others cite the hectic schedules of both Jesus and Nicodemus and the fact that the after hours visit offered a greater promise of an uninterrupted conversation. Some have simply reasoned that Nicodemus was timid and was seeking an inconspicuous time for an interview. The significant truth is that Nicodemus was inquiring of the one person in all of human history who could help him most.

When Nicodemus came to Jesus on that night long ago, he did not need religion. The Bible specifically states that Nicodemus was a Pharisee, and the Pharisees were intensely religious. They were up to their necks in religion. There were never more than six thousand Pharisees at any one time and they all made vows to obey every Jewish law. Hundreds of these laws came from several sources (the Old Testament, the Mishnah, and the Talmud). The Pharisees were committed to keeping every law in the most meticulous way to the minutest detail.

An example of the hyper-legalism of the Pharisees is the endless regulations they made about the observance of the Sabbath day. The Bible says that this hallowed day is to be kept sacred. It was given to man for rest and worship; no work was to be done on the Sabbath. The Pharisees were not at all content with such generalizations concerning the observance of the Sabbath day. Therefore, they spent years defining work and making lists of things prohibited on the Lord's Day.

Examples abound in the Mishnah, a collection of decisions made by rabbis, which had twenty-four chapters on the observance of the Sabbath. It was specified that making knots should be considered work, unless, of course, they could be tied or untied with one hand. The carrying of a burden was defined as any food weighing more than a dried fig or any milk exceeding one swallow. The Pharisaical law specified that an egg laid on the Sabbath could be eaten if you killed the chicken the next day as punishment for laying an egg on the day of rest. A woman was not permitted to look in a mirror on the Sabbath day. The reason for such legislation was that she might see a gray hair and be tempted to pull it out. Removing one hair from the head was considered work and a desecration of the holy day. Some believe that dentures and wooden legs came under the classification of burdens and, therefore, could not be worn on the Sabbath day because of the stipulation against bearing burdens on that day.

The point is that the Pharisees were hyper-legalists who externalized religion. They had a form of godliness, but they denied the power thereof (2 Tim.3:5). Jesus indicted the Pharisees for majoring on minors and neglecting the important issues of life such as judgment, mercy, and faith (see Matt. 23:23). He said, "You will strain at a gnat and swallow a camel" (Matt. 23:24). There was no reality, no vitality, and no authenticity to the religion of the Pharisees.

There are many people in the world today like the Pharisees. They are religious, but lost. They are moral, ethical, honest, law abiding citizens; but they do not have a personal relationship with Jesus Christ. Many of these people are in the church, but their lives have never been transformed by the power of God. What our world needs today is not more religion. We have enough religion already. The devil himself is not opposed to religion. Satan will allow a man to be religious and, in fact, promote religion if that religion will keep a man from Christ.

Nicodemus did not need religion, but he obviously needed something. He came to Jesus in search of that something which he needed to fill the void in his life. He had a hunger for something more than the voluminous rules and regulations of an empty religion. Perhaps Nicodemus had observed Jesus from a distance. He had heard of the miracles that Jesus had performed. Somehow Nicodemus knew that Jesus was more than a charlatan exploiting the gullibility of the lame, the halt, and the blind. He came to Jesus recognizing that there was something different, something special about him. He said, "Rabbi, we know that thou art a teacher come from God: for no man can do these miracles that thou doest, except God be with him" (v. 2).

Nicodemus had come to the right person. In Jesus he was about to discover the answer to all his questions. He was about to find the key to unlock the door that religion would not unlock.

The Advocacy Of The New Birth

The first words of Jesus to Nicodemus were: "Verily, Verily I say unto thee, except a man be born again, he cannot see the kingdom of God" (v.3). Up until this point no one had said one word about "the kingdom of God." What is Jesus talking about? Is He answering a question nobody's asking? Absolutely not! Jesus knew exactly what Nicodemus was thinking.

In fact, look at the last two verses of the preceding chapter in John's Gospel: "But Jesus did not commit himself unto them, because he knew all men, and needed not that any should testify of man: for he knew what was in him" (Jn. 2:24-25). Now notice that the next chapter begins in the original language with a word, which is often omitted in translation or simply rendered, "now." Another translation for this word is "but," and such a word choice seems more appropriate because Nicodemus seems to stand in direct opposition to the superficial commitment and the shallow thinking of those who profess to believe on Jesus in John 2. Jesus knew what was in man and He had already seen in Nicodemus a certain honest searching that set him apart from the rest.

So when Jesus brought up "the kingdom of God" he was not ignoring Nicodemus' question; he was going straight to the issue of supreme importance. He introduced Nicodemus to the principle of the new birth. In essence, Jesus said, "Nicodemus, there is a life of freedom and abundance and purpose awaiting you. God is not in a system of inconsequential rules and regulations. He is not in worn out customs and musty traditions. He is a present living reality, but to know Him in an intimate, personal way, you must be born again." In this passage of Scripture, John, for the first time from the lips of Jesus, gives the plan of salvation.

The "kingdom of God" actually signifies the whole sphere of salvation. It is a reference to God's world, the world of those who have been redeemed. F. B. Meyer calls this present world "the kingdom of the flesh." Indeed, "that which is born of flesh is flesh...." (Jn. 3:6). But, "above this kingdom," Meyer says, "there is another--the kingdom of the spiritual and eternal. This is the supreme realm of life, the element and home of God." [7] So Jesus starts out by telling Nicodemus that there is a whole other realm of reality for which he must search.

How do you search for a kingdom you can't see? The Greek word for "see" is "eidon" which means "to know or to experience." So, in order to get the full impact of Jesus' words to Nicodemus, consider this paraphrase: "Except a man be born again he cannot understand or comprehend the things of God." Paul underscored this truth in his first Corinthian epistle when he writes: "But the natural man receiveth not the things of the Spirit of God: for they are foolishness unto him: neither can he know them because they are spiritually discerned" (1 Cor. 2:14). The unbeliever is groping in spiritual blindness and is not able to comprehend God's truth. However, when the Spirit of God draws a man to conversion, the light of spiritual understanding breaks forth. Nicodemus needed the new birth to have his eyes opened and the kingdom revealed to him.

On July 2, 1990, a terrible electrical storm hit Jackson, Mississippi, at about sundown. The storm was accompanied by terrific gusts of wind. Trees fell! Power lines were downed! Streets were scattered with limbs and debris! Homes were damaged, some destroyed! I was at home on that fateful evening with our twin sons. My wife, Martha Jean, was in the Atlanta area looking for a house for us to purchase pursuant of my call to the Peachtree Corners Baptist Church in Norcross, Georgia. In the midst of the storm, Martha Jean called to announce, "I have found three houses I really like. Could you come and help me make a final decision?" Then she added, "When you come, bring my black split skirt and my black and white shoes."

Considering the storm, I thought I'd just fly to Atlanta the next morning, but our sons, John and Jerry, insisted that they help with the "big" decision, so we all decided to jump into the car and head out for Atlanta as soon as possible. At that moment the storm outside reached its fiercest moment. The lightning flashed through the semi-darkness. An electrical transformer nearby "popped" and we were instantly deprived of our electricity. I could not find a candle or even a match. As one might well suspect, the batteries in the flashlight were old and ineffective. The closet in our bedroom was as dark as a cypress swamp at midnight. I opened the closet door toward the window and tried to use the occasional flashes of lightning to aid me in selecting my wardrobe for the trip. I groped and grasped and gasped and grimaced through that closet trying to determine the clothes that I needed by feeling the texture of the fabric and trying to determine the design. I quickly realized that I was incapable of verifying anything. The possibility of getting Martha Jean's black split skirt in a closet where everything was black was impossible. I was in total darkness until the boys found an emergency light in the trunk of their car. When that light illuminated that closet it was like a revelation. The light changed everything.

The new birth is like that emergency light – it makes the impossible possible. It enables a man to see, to know, and to comprehend the kingdom of God.

But to the person who wants to enter the kingdom of God, the new birth is not optional. Neither is it just advisable or somewhat commendable . It is absolutely imperative. Remember in verse 5, our Lord said, "...except a man be born of water and of the Spirit he cannot enter into the kingdom of God." Jesus passionately declared in verse 7, "Marvel not that I said unto thee. Ye must be born again." He is as emphatic as Nicodemus is baffled.

Imagine the startled look on the face of Nicodemus when he heard Jesus speak of the imperative of the new birth. Imagine his disappointment. He wasn't in his religion for the fun of it—in fact, there was no fun in being a Pharisee. They were known for their fasting and long faces. He was earnestly seeking the kingdom of God. When Jesus said, "You must be born again," essentially he was saying, "Add up all your worn out traditions and ancient festivals and solemn sacrifices and bias platitudes and finicky laws, and you will find out you are one big, fat, Pharisaical zero. None of it, nor all of it combined, will get you into the kingdom of God. You must be born anew. Nicodemus, you've got to scrap everything and start all over again."

People are always making resolutions to do better, to change, only to break those resolutions soon afterward; but the Bible teaches us that through the new birth we can enter a new world. Billy Graham has often stated, "The new birth is not just being reformed; it's being transformed." Through Ezekiel, the Old Testament prophet, God said, "A new heart also will I give you, and a new spirit will I put within you: and I will take away the stony heart out of your flesh, and I will give you a heart of flesh. And I will put my spirit within you, and cause you to walk in my statutes, and ye shall keep my judgments, and do them" (Ez. 36:26-27). A man with a new life, a new birth, a new heart, and a new spirit is a man who is radically changed.

Entering the kingdom begins with a new birth and ends with a total transformation. How is it done?

The Agents Of The New Birth

In life and throughout the Bible, there are multiplied illustrations of those in whom God wrought a radical change. Saul met Jesus on the road to Damascus and was born again. His life was changed when he met the Stranger of Galilee. Saul became Paul and was never the same again. He became a crusader for Christ. He loved the Lord. Nicodemus, like Paul, needed to be born again.

In verse 5 of John 3, Jesus mentions the two agents or instruments of the new birth. He insists that "...a man be born of water and of the spirit...." What does Jesus mean when He speaks of being "born of water?" There has been considerable speculation as to the meaning of this term "born of water."

When Jesus spoke of water, Nicodemus' first thought must have been of the water in the Old Testament used for purification. The Jewish people had specified under their law that if a person or an object was unclean or defiled, a ceremonial washing of water was necessary. For example, the Levites were used in the Lord's service and the Lord instructed Moses to sprinkle them with the "water of purifying" (see Num. 8:7). In Numbers 19 we have the Old Testament ordinances for the purification of the unclean: "And a man that is clean shall gather up the ashes of the heifer, and lay them up without the camp in a clean place, and it shall be kept for the congregation of the children of Israel for a water of separation: it is a purification for sin" (Num. 19:17). Such a ceremonial washing of water would have been an insult to Nicodemus because that rite was the avenue by which an unclean Gentile could become a member of the Jewish faith. However, in light of other scripture, we can be certain that the phrase "born of water" is not a reference to the "water of purification" used for ceremonial cleansing in the Old Testament.

There are those who believe that the phrase "born of water" is a reference to physical birth. Nicodemus must have considered this interpretation as well, yet his physical birth was a foregone conclusion. Having already been born physically, he could not have repeated that experience. In fact, he asked, "How can a man be born when he is old? Can he enter the second time into his mother's womb and be born" (v. 4)? So, the phrase "born of water" is not a reference to physical birth.

There are others who believe that being "born of water" is a reference to the baptism of John, the forerunner of Jesus. In fact, the Bible declares: "John did baptize in the wilderness, and preached the baptism of repentance for the remission of sins" (Mark 1:4). Honestly, I rather like the idea of a correlation between the phrase "born of water" and John's "baptism of repentance." Repentance was the topic of the first message that Jesus preached (see Matt.4:17). In the last message of Jesus, He emphasized the need for repentance (see Rev. 3:19). In the Bible the command to repent is issued in some form or other 969 times. The Greek word for "repentance" is "metanoia" which means a complete change of mind and a reversal of direction. It signifies not only a change of mind about your sins, but it signifies a change of mind about God, who is the remedy for sin.

Perhaps the most beautiful illustration of repentance in the Bible is found in the story of the prodigal son. This rebellious young man had plummeted to the depths of sin. He had sunk down into the quagmire of degradation and was in a deplorable situation. Then it was that he came to his senses and said, "I will arise and go to my father, and will say unto him, 'Father, I have sinned against heaven and before thee...'" Luke 15:18. Herein is repentance, and there is no regeneration apart from it.

Please remember that Nicodemus was a Pharisee and consequently a meticulous keeper of the law. Any suggestion that he needed to repent was surely repugnant to him. The very thought of repentance was humiliating. Yet, Jesus said, "I tell you, nay: but, except you repent, ye shall all likewise perish" (Lk. 13:3). Repentance is not just necessary for the one who overtly rebels against God, but for all men. However, as much as I like the seeming correlation between the phrase "born of water" and John's "baptism of repentance," there seems to be no evidence whatsoever that the two are analogous. In fact, John the Baptist said, "I, indeed, baptize you with water unto repentance: but he that cometh after me is mightier than I, whose shoes I am not worthy to bear: He shall baptize you with the Holy Ghost and with fire" (Matt. 3:11).

Finally, there are some who think that the phrase "born of water" is a reference to baptismal regeneration and therefore, you have to be baptized in water in order to be saved. This belief runs counter to the clear, Biblical principle taught in Ephesians 2:8-9: "For by grace are ye saved through faith; and that not of yourselves: it is the gift of God: Not of works, lest any many should boast." Water produces no spiritual cleansing. No one is saved by an external bath.

Water baptism is a symbol--a significant symbol, but only a symbol. It symbolizes the fact that the new convert has been baptized by the Holy Spirit. The baptism of the Holy Spirit is a one-time experience that happens at the moment of salvation. The baptism of a new believer into the local, visible church portrays the baptism of the Holy Spirit that places the new Christian into the eternal, invisible church. Baptism by immersion also symbolizes the new believer's identification with Christ in His death, burial, and resurrection. It is a pictorial testimony whereby the child of God affirms that he believes "that Christ died for our sins... and that He was buried, and that He arose again on the third day according to the Scriptures" (1 Cor. 15:3-4). Furthermore, baptism is an emblem of the believer's being "dead indeed unto sin, but alive unto God through Jesus Christ our Lord" (Rom. 6:11). The apostle Paul declares that in baptism "...we are buried with Him by baptism into death: that like as Christ was raised up from the dead by the glory of the Father, even so we also should walk in newness of life" (Rom. 6:4). I also believe that this ordinance pictures the physical death of the saint of God as he is lowered beneath the water. His emerging from the water portrays the resurrection of the body at the rapture of the church.

So what is this water to which Jesus refers? I believe Jesus used the word "water" to refer to the Word of God. Water is frequently used in the Bible to symbolize or represent the Word of God. Isaiah wrote, "For as the rain cometh down, and the snow from heaven, and returneth not thither, but watereth the earth, and maketh it bring forth and bud, that it may give seed to the sower, and bread to the eater: so shall my word be that goeth forth out of my mouth: it shall not return unto me void, but it shall accomplish that which I please, and it shall prosper in the thing whereunto I send it" (Is. 55:10-11).

So, water symbolizes the Word of God. This holy Word is one of the agents of purification and regeneration. For example, the Psalmist asks, "Wherewithal shall a young man cleanse his way?" He answers his own question by replying, "By taking heed thereto according to thy word" (Ps.119:9). To His disciples, Jesus said, "Now ye are clean through the word which I have spoken unto you" (Jn. 15:3). To the Ephesian Christians the apostle Paul indicated that Christ was forever sanctifying and cleansing the church "with the washing of water by the word" (Eph.5:26). The Word of God is the agent of cleansing.

Furthermore, the Bible declares that we are quickened by the Word of God (see Ps.119:50), begotten by the Word of truth (see James 1:18), and born again by the incorruptible Word of God (see 1 Pet. 1:23). James, in his epistle, says, "The engrafted word...is able to save your souls" (1:21).

Dr. W. A. Criswell of First Baptist Church, Dallas, Texas, tells about the young cowboy out in West Texas who heard the Word of God and was saved. There was a foreman on a west Texas ranch who was a Christian and faithfully tried to win his cowboys to faith in Jesus Christ. When the day's work was done, he would gather his cowboys around the campfire, and he would read to them out of God's Book, and tell them about the incomparable love of Jesus.

One day during the fall round-up a horse lost his foothold and fell over backwards on top of its rider. The horse got up and stumbled away, but when the cowboy tried to get up he was crushed internally, was bleeding profusely from the mouth, and couldn't rise.

The cook in the camp saw what had happened and he ran over to the young lad, picked him up, and carried him back to the camp. The young cowboy was gently placed on a cot. As the young man's life ebbed away, he turned to the cook and said, "Jake, you know that big, black Book the foreman is always reading to us? Would you get it, Jake, and being it to me?"

Immediately, the cook went to the chuck wagon and among the things of the foreman he found the big, black Bible. He brought it to the dying cowboy who said to the cook, "Jake, you know that verse that the foreman is always reading to us—John 3:16? Could you please find that verse?"

The cook opened the Bible and fumbled through its pages until he found the Gospel of John and the requested verse. The young cowboy then said, "Jake, read to me that verse."

The cook read out of the foreman's Bible, "For God so loved the world that He gave His only begotten Son, that whosoever believeth on Him should not perish, but have everlasting life."

With his life fading away, the young cowboy said, "That's it, Jake. Now, would you please take that Bible and put it on my chest and would you take my finger and put it on that verse? Jake, when the foreman comes in to eat, will you tell him that I died with my finger on John 3:16?"

"One glad smile of pleasure
O'er the cowboy's face was spread.
One dark, convulsive shadow,
And the tall, young lad was dead.

Far from his home and family,

They laid him down to rest
With a saddle for a pillow,
And that Bible on his chest." [8]

The cowboy understood what Jesus was sharing with Nicodemus, that he needed to be "born of water and of the spirit" (v.5). The Spirit of God uses the testimony of the Word of God to bring men to salvation. As one preacher said, "The Holy Spirit of God is the begetter; the Word is the 'seed' He uses." The Holy Spirit is the catalyst that joins the engrafted Word to the heart of man, producing the new birth—the breath of God that quickens and enlivens.

Even as the Holy Spirit planted the seed of God inside the Virgin Mary to produce the physical birth of Christ, so does He implant the seed of the Word into our lives to produce the Spiritual birth. Our Savior said, "It is the spirit (wind, breath) that giveth life: the flesh profiteth nothing" (Jn 6:63). The apostle Paul affirms this in his letter to Titus: "Not by works of righteousness which we have done, but according to his mercy he saved us, by the washing of regeneration, and the renewing of the Holy Spirit" (Titus 3:5). The water and the Spirit, the Word and the wind, are the agents of the new birth.

The Analogy Of The New Birth

To conclude his conversation with Nicodemus, Jesus draws an analogy between the operation of the Holy Spirit and the wind: "The wind bloweth where it listeth, and thou hearest the sound thereof, but canst not tell whence it cometh, and whether it goeth: so is everyone that is born of the Spirit." Please remember that the Greek word "pneuma" can be translated "spirit," "breath," and "wind." The metaphor of the wind is an appropriate symbol of the Holy Spirit because it illustrates the way He works to provide salvation.

Notice first the exercise of the wind in bringing salvation. Jesus said, "The wind bloweth." The Holy Spirit is busy exercising His ministry in our world today. Like the wind currents, this third person of the Trinity remains in constant motion. At the very dawn of creation the Spirit of God "moved upon the face of the waters" (Gen. 1:2). Then the Bible declares that "the Spirit of God came upon Balaam" (Num. 24:2). The Spirit of God also came upon Saul (1 Sam.10:10), upon the messengers of Saul (1 Sam. 19:20), upon Azariah (2 Chron.15:1), and upon Simeon (Lk. 2:25).

Furthermore, the Holy Spirit strives with sinners (Gen. 6:3). He calls (Acts 13:2); He intercedes (Rom. 8:26); He searches (1 Cor. 2:10); He quickens (Jn. 6:63); He helps our infirmities (Rom. 8:26); He leads (Gal. 5:18); He bears witness (1 Jn. 5:6); He gives power (Acts 1:8); He sanctifies (1 Pet. 1:2); He teaches (Jn. 14:26); He convicts of sin, righteousness, and judgment (Jn. 16:8). The Holy Spirit is actively involved in the work of redemption today.

However, it is possible for a man to so resist the Holy Spirit and so completely heed the call of the world that the Spirit of God determines no longer to strive with him (see Gen. 6:3). Furthermore, the day is coming when the church is going to be raptured, and the Holy Spirit, who is the restrainer of evil and the agent of salvation, will be removed from the earth at that time. When the saints go marching into glory, the Holy Spirit, who is the earnest of our inheritance, will deliver us to the Lord Jesus Christ and present us to Him. Then the Spirit of God will come back to the earth, but His mission will be different. We do not know all that He will do in those days following the rapture of the church, but He will not hinder evil. He will let the devil have his day for a while (see 2 Thess. 2:6).

Before we move forward in our consideration of the new birth, I think it well to pause and consider that God might be speaking to you at this moment. Indeed, if God is breathing these truths into your conscience, it is imperative that you respond to the activity of the Holy Spirit in this day of grace and opportunity. If the wind of the Spirit is stirring in your soul, let its gentle breeze carry you into God's saving grace.

Let us now notice not only the exercise of the wind, but also the emancipation of the wind. Jesus said, "...the wind bloweth where it listeth...." The wind, like the Spirit, is its own master: it is impossible for man to tame or to control. Thus it is rather foolish to try to fashion our little plans for the kingdom and ask God to send His wind of blessing upon them. Instead, we should be seeking the face of God, seeking to understand His will, and the direction in which the wind of the Spirit is blowing and just get in on what God is up to.

Years ago Jack Taylor wrote a book entitled, *Victory over the Devil.* In the book he coins the word "theodynamics." The Greek word, "theos" means God; the Greek word "dunamis" signifies power. "Theodynamics," therefore, stands for "God power."

Taylor proposes that God is God everywhere and that God is working as God everywhere. [9] Of course, the evidences of God's work are variable because we often, by our disobedience, quench the Holy Spirit. Nevertheless, somehow we must apply the principles of theodynamics to our lives so that we are living in the stream of God's mighty power. We must get in the wind currents of God's activity. If we fail to do so, we will be drifting in the doldrums where worlds of self-effort produce nothing.

Having resided and pastored in Jackson, Mississippi for more than a decade, I am somewhat familiar with the problem of flooding. The Pearl River has been known to overflow its banks and produce great devastation. Levees have been built to contain the rising water at the time of a flood, but occasionally the levees are not high enough or extensive enough to provide the needed protection. The 1979 Easter Flood in Jackson was particularly destructive as the water rose above the levees just south of the city and portions of downtown Jackson became submerged. Interestingly, the rising water lifted one boat on the Pearl River up, up, up and, when the water level began to subside, the old wooden fishing boat was left on top of the levee. For years this remnant of the '79 flood stood as a silent monument to the havoc wrought by that natural disaster. By and by, the paint started to peel off, and the boards started to spring out from the sides of the boat. The effect of the sun and the wind on the old vessel became more and more evident. The greatest problem with the fishing boat, however, was that on its lofty perch atop the levee, it was out of touch with the stream.

Similarly, I fear that we get out of touch with the person and the ministry of the Holy Spirit. Instead of getting in on what God is up to, we try to fit the Spirit of God into our puny plans, our self-styled systems, and our ordinary organizations. We must cease from trying to put God in a box and begin to yield to His sovereignty so that the Spirit is set free and emancipated in our lives.

The Bible says, "Where the Spirit of the Lord is, there is liberty" (2 Cor.3:17). When we thus yield to the Spirit of the Living God, we get in on the wind currents of His mighty activity. I believe that when a church is living in obedience to God and surrendered to the Spirit, there is no remnant of self and no region of sin beyond His power to redeem. There is no winter death of the soul that He cannot quicken into a blossoming springtime of life and no valley of dry bones he cannot vitalize into a marching army. This is the glory of Pentecost.

In fact, I would say that the church which has neglected its call to get into the flow of God's Spirit ought to find out where the Spirit of God is working and invest as much of its personnel and as much of its resources in that operation of the Spirit as possible. Dead churches that are void of influence and power, that seldom, if ever, see a soul saved, that have drifted into a Laodicean complacency, ought to be honest enough to recognize their woeful condition and get right with God. If they are not willing to do that, they ought to sell their property and their buildings, liquidate their assets, and send the money to Africa or China or Korea, where God has set His Spirit free to do a mighty work.

There is also the evidence of the wind. While yu can see neither the wind nor the Spirit, you can see the evidence of both. Jesus reminds Nicodemus of the evidence of the wind: "...the wind bloweth where it listed, and thou heareth the sound thereof...." Quite often at night when I go to bed, I can hear the wind whistling through the evergreen trees in our backyard. The wind is announcing its presence. The work and ministry of the Holy Spirit is similar. Sometimes the work of the Spirit is like a gentle zephyr blowing so softly it scarcely rustles a leaf while at other times it rushes in as a storm.

Do you remember Lydia of Thyatira? When the apostle Paul met Lydia, she was in Philippi and had joined herself with other women down by the riverside. These women were having a prayer meeting. The Bible suggests that though she worshiped God and spent time in prayer, she was not saved. However, as Paul spoke to Lydia that day concerning the Lord Jesus Christ, the gentle breeze of the Spirit warmed her heart. The Bible simply reports that her heart was opened and "she attended unto the things which were spoken of Paul. And...she was baptized, and her household...." (Acts 16:14-15a).

Then Lydia said to Paul and Silas, "If ye have judged me to be faithful to the Lord, come into my house and abide there" (Acts 16:15b). In other words, she said, "If you see any evidence of the Spirit working in my life and in the life of my family, we'd love to have some Christian fellowship." Apparently, the evidence of the new birth was there, because in Acts 16:40, we are told that they "entered into the house of Lydia." There was no tornado, no lightning, no thunderbolts, no mighty upheaval surrounding the conversion of Lydia; but the tranquil breeze of the Spirit had swept through her heart and the evidence was there.

In Acts 2, the Spirit came not as a gentle breeze, but as "a rushing mighty wind" (Acts 2:2). There was ample evidence of the Spirit's working on that occasion. In that dramatic moment the believers were filled with the Holy Spirit. They were ignited with divine power. Cloven tongues of fire appeared and sat upon each of them. The believers were gifted to speak in other languages and thus communicate God's truth to people of different lands. There was a change in their demeanor and personality (see Acts 2:15-21). The people reacted to this phenomenon in amazement. Some doubted and some mocked at these disciples, who were inhabited by the Spirit. They were all ignited with divine power. When Peter preached that day, three thousand souls were saved.

Just like the wind, when the Spirit of God moves, there is evidence of it. Hungry souls congregate to hear God's truth. The church is revived. Faith is renewed. Saints are encouraged. Sinners are convicted of their wickedness. Souls are saved.

There is a mystery about the wind. Its origin is unknown. Jesus said, "Thou hearest the sound thereof . . . but thou canst not tell whence it cometh." Likewise, there is a mystery about the operations of the Holy Spirit.

Do you remember when Jesus was with His disciples at Caesarea Philippi? He asked them, "Whom do men say that I, the Son of man, am?" (Matt.16:13). The disciples responded by saying, "Some say that thou art John the Baptist; some Elijah; and others, Jeremiah, or one of the prophets" (v. 14).

Then Jesus made His question more direct. He said, "But whom say ye that I am?" (v.15).

Peter, impetuous as he was, gave his classic, beautiful response, "Thou art the Christ, the Son of the Living God" (v.16). As soon as Peter gave his answer, he must have looked around and asked, "Where did that come from?" It was beyond Peter to give such an accurate, definitive answer and he knew it.

Jesus said to Peter, "Blessed art thou, Simon Bar-Jona: for flesh and blood hath not revealed it unto thee, but my Father which is in heaven" (v. 17).

We may not know the origin of the wind or how the Spirit gains entrance into our lives, but we do know that His operations are directed from above. They come from wherever God is. We don't work up the new birth or devise our own salvation. The apostle John said, "But as many as receive Him (Christ), to them gave He power to become the sons of God, even to them that believe on His name: which were born, not of blood nor of the will of the flesh, nor of the will of man, but of God" (Jn. 1:12-13). Nor can we concoct a revival or conjure up a spiritual renewal in the energy of the flesh. The Spirit does not gain entrance into the life of the church through self-effort. The Word of the Lord came to Zerubbabel in the Old Testament, saying, "Not by might, nor by power, but by my Spirit, saith the Lord of hosts" (Zech. 4:6). We may not know the direction from which the wind or the spirit comes, but we know that each comes from God and thus mysteriously gains entrance into our lives.

Finally, there is the need to consider the extent of the wind, because we are incapable of determining the extent to which the wind or the spirit might take us. Jesus said, "Thou canst not tell whence it cometh, and whether it goeth: so is everyone that is born of the Spirit."

In 1874, a small group of people gathered in Swan Quarter, North Carolina, to construct a church building. They were not able to build their church upon the plot of ground, which they desired for their location because they were unable to purchase it. However, on September 17, 1876, a terrific storm with raging winds struck that part of eastern North Carolina. The church building was lifted up by the wind and carried a distance of 300 feet and miraculously set down intact upon the property, which the members had earnestly desired to be the location for their church. That church building stands today on that exact plot of ground, which apparently God had ultimately ordained for their location. [10]

No one can tell where the Holy Spirit may lead the yielded believer in this life before God calls him home. We do not know that Nicodemus was saved that night when Jesus pressed upon him the importance of the new birth, but I do believe that there was a time in the life of Nicodemus when he experienced the breath that births and was caught up in the wind of God's Spirit. Do you remember where it took him?

In John 7, the wind of the Spirit drove Nicodemus to stand up in defense of Jesus before the rulers of the Pharisees. It appears that Nicodemus chose to stand as a disciple of Jesus amidst the powerful religious machinery of his day. For his defense of Jesus that day, he received the ridicule of the Sanhedrin who scornfully asked him if he was also a Galilean (see Jn. 7:50-52). In another daring act of loyalty to Christ, Nicodemus, along with Joseph of Arimathaea, entered the counsel chamber of Pilate to ask for the body of Jesus. The wind of the Spirit had carried Nicodemus from that clandestine meeting with Jesus on a darkened night to places of daring and danger for the cause of his Savior.

The point is that when you pray for the leadership of the Holy Spirit, He may lead you into dramatic and even dangerous steps of faith and commitment. Are you willing for the Spirit of God to take you where He will? Are you willing to launch out into the deep with Him to attempt mighty exploits for God regardless of the cost or the cross involved? Isn't it time the people of God were driven by the wind of the Spirit to bring glory to God?

"Will God ever ask you to do something you are not able to do? The answer is yes — all the time! It must be that way, for God's glory and kingdom. If we function according to our ability alone, we get the glory; if we function according to the power of the Spirit within us, God gets the glory. He wants to reveal Himself to a watching world." [11]

Henry T. Blackaby

Holy Exhalation
John 20:19-23

Fremantle Media began production of an all-new version of the old television game show, "Let's Make a Deal." Martha Jean and I were on the antiquated version of the show in 1967. Monty Hall was the host and master of ceremonies. The programs were taped ine Burbank, California. While on a trip to California, my wife and I went to the network studios to try to get on the audience participation show where great prizes were often awarded to lucky contestants.

Amazingly, we were chosen out of hundreds of potential candidates to be contestants on the show. Furthermore, we won a Maytag washer and dryer, $200 and a year's supply of Borax detergent and qualified to participate in the final event for the grand prize. The curtain was opened, and there was the prize—a beautiful, bright, shiny, red Pontiac Firebird convertible—the perfect car for a Baptist preacher!

We got a set of keys out of three possible choices. Monty Hall said, "You can keep your washer and dryer and $200, and give me back the keys or you can give up the prizes you have already won and try your keys to see if they will open the door to the new car. One of the sets of keys fits the red convertible. If the key you've chosen opens the door to the car, you've won our grand prize for today's show."

What would you have done? My whole life passed before my eyes in a split second. I could see myself driving that car to the associational pastors' conference and parking between two old "clunkers" owned by some of the other preachers. I could see myself in that bright, sporty model following the hearse in a funeral procession. I could see myself driving that car and thus inviting an early mid-life crisis at age 26. I could see my wife, Martha Jean, getting the "Firebird" and me being stuck with the '61 Ford Falcon.

I looked at Monty Hall and said, "We'll keep what we've got," and I handed the keys back to him.

In our text we read that Jesus breathed on the disciples and said, "Receive ye the Holy Spirit." That holy exhalation was somewhat like the car keys Monty Hall gave us, except in the breath of Jesus there were no catches, no tricks, no gimmicks, no risks, no possibility of hopes being dashed on the rocks of disappointment.

When we selected those keys out of the three sets of keys, we knew that we had only a one-in-three chance of winning a car. Furthermore, we already had something in our hands, which we stood the possibility of having to forfeit if we failed to choose the right key. It was risky business.

When Jesus breathed upon the disciples, He gave them the keys to the Holy Spirit—the pledge that the Spirit would come, the absolute assurance that the Spirit of God would be their holy inhabitor. The text doesn't say that they received the Holy Spirit at that moment, but I do believe that they received the promise, the guarantee, that He would soon be an ever-present, indwelling reality. Perhaps they even received a foretaste of what they were about to receive in fullness. By the way, the key we chose for the car didn't fit the ignition, so we were able to go home as happy recipients of the lesser prizes.

Let us consider what the text has to report about this post-resurrection appearance of Jesus to His anxious, waiting disciples.

The Appearance Of Jesus

The Moment Of His Appearing

Now, as we consider the appearance of Jesus, let us notice first the moment of His appearing. Picture the scene described in the Scripture verses before us. It is the first day of the week—the evening of the day that Jesus arose from the dead. Mary Magdalene had been the first one to visit the sepulcher that day. Before the breaking of the dawn, she had gone to the burial place of Jesus only to discover that the stone had been rolled away from the entrance of the grave and that the body of Jesus was missing. She immediately informed Peter and John, who hurriedly ran to the tomb to conduct their own investigation. They, too, found the sepulcher empty and the grave clothes of Jesus neatly folded and laid aside. Later that morning, Mary Magdalene saw two angels in the tomb, but as she turned to leave the burial place she saw the resurrected

Lord. Mary then became the first herald of the resurrection. She found the disciples and declared, "I have seen the Lord!"

Apparently, the resurrection of Jesus caught the disciples by surprise. You would have thought the disciples would have been nodding their heads as they went down their checklist of all the things Jesus foretold. On numerous occasions Jesus spoke of His impending death and subsequent resurrection (see Matt. 16:21-26; 17:22-23; 20:17-19; 26:31-32). Jesus had even specified the day of His betrayal (see Matt. 26:1-5). Furthermore, Jesus predicted Peter's denial (Matt. 26:33-35) and unmasked Judas as the betrayer (Matt. 26:20-25). The events of recent days had happened according to Old Testament prophecy and the sayings of Jesus.

The disciples, however, seemed to be astounded and mystified by all that had transpired. In fact, the Scriptures declare in John 20:9, "For as yet they knew not the Scripture that He must rise again from the dead." The truth is that John, the beloved disciple, had to see the empty tomb in order to be convinced of the resurrection (see Jn. 20:8).

That first resurrection Sunday was an action-packed, heart-challenging, mind-boggling, history-making, life-changing day. As the sun set, the disciples were gathered in solemn assembly. Notice the text: "Then the same day at evening, being the first day of the week, when the doors were shut where the disciples were assembled for fear of the Jews, came Jesus and stood in the midst...." (v. 19). This verse denotes the moment of His appearance. The Holy Spirit is careful to note that this gathering of disciples was on the first day of the week.

The resurrection changed the whole economy of worship because historically believers no longer worshipped on the Sabbath or the seventh day of the week, but on the day of the resurrection, the first day of the week. From this point on to the end of the New Testament, the first day of the week was known as the Lord's Day, the day of worship, the day to retreat from the cares of the world and focus upon the things of God (see Acts 20:7; 1 Cor. 16:1-2; and, Rev. 1:10).

One of the mightiest tools that the devil is using to decimate the church and the work of God is the secularization of Sunday. In my own lifetime, I have seen God's holy day become a holiday or just another day in the week with very little distinctiveness. There are very few people in our society who devote the entire Lord's Day to the One who is worthy of worship. Robert Murray McCheyne said, "Did you ever meet with a lively believer in any country under heaven--one who loved Christ, and lived a holy life--who did not delight in keeping holy to God the entire Lord's Day?" [12]

I thank God for men like Truett Cathey, the founder of Chick-Fil-A, who has determined that his restaurants are not going to be open on Sunday. Yet I am quite sure that he has one of the most successful food service businesses in the country. He is a committed Christian, and he is determined to honor the Lord's Day with his life and with his business. Dwight L. Moody said, "You show me a nation that has given up the Sabbath and I will show you a nation that has got the seeds of decay." [13]

Occasionally, certain people will excuse their absence from church by saying, "Sunday is the only day that I have." My thought is, "No, Sunday is the only day that you really do not have. It is the

Lord's day." Ignatius, one of the early Christian leaders, said, "Let everyone that loveth Christ keep holy the first day of the week, the Lord's Day." [14] Sunday is the queen of all days. It is God's gift to us. When we are tired and discouraged from daily toil, from rushing to and fro, from encountering busy traffic, crowded stores, a competitive world, and tensions and pressures, Sunday comes and we can slow down, relax, rest, and worship God and be renewed in strength, courage, and spirit. I believe that by being in God's house, as we ought on God's day, we have our strength renewed like the strength of an eagle.

The fact that the disciples were gathered on Sunday evening and that Jesus appeared to them, presents a good case for the Sunday evening worship service. More and more we hear of church buildings that are dark on Sunday night. Sunday evening is a good time to gather the church, edify the saints, glorify the Son, and demonstrate to the world that we are seeking first the kingdom of God and His righteousness. Poor Thomas, the doubting disciple, was absent when Jesus appeared to the disciples on that first Easter Sunday evening. Think of all that poor Thomas missed by not being present for that time of affirmation and praise and fellowship with the Lord.

The Miracle Of His Appearing

However, notice not only the moment of His appearing, but also the miracle of His appearing. Our text says that the disciples were gathered in this room, and "the doors were shut." The Greek word signifies that they were "barred shut." At this point they were not singing songs of praise and experiencing glorious worship. They were huddled behind barricaded doors, petrified with fear because of the Jews. They were probably wondering, "Who's going to be crucified next?"

Then, into the midst of those fearful disciples, Jesus appeared. What a fantastic thought! But, how did Jesus manage to enter the room with the doors locked and barred? There are those who are always trying to rationalize away the miracles of the Bible. They have presented their theories about this post-resurrection appearance of Jesus. There are some who contend that what the disciples saw was a phantom or an apparition. Others say that Jesus descended from the roof or climbed through a window. It has also been suggested that the doorkeeper let Jesus in when no one was watching and then denied it. I find quite interesting the theory that asserts that Jesus was in the room hiding in a corner and then suddenly appeared at the appropriate time. It is an interesting theory, but I doubt Jesus was interested in playing "hide and seek" with the disciples on that occasion.

I believe, however, that the glorified body of Jesus was so uniquely designed that after the resurrection He knew no limitations of time, space, or matter. His miraculous manifestation to the disciples on that occasion introduced a new order of existence. This remarkable body of Jesus had the capacity to appear or disappear. Jesus could then rearrange the molecules in the wall and walk through it unhindered. Prior to His death He walked on the water. Why should it now be so surprising that He could walk through a wall? I believe that He also had the capacity to travel at the speed of thought.

Later on His ascension proved that His glorified body was not subject to the laws of gravity. Yet, Jesus' body could be touched and felt, and He had the capacity to consume food (see Lk. 24:39-43). The promise of God's Word is that one day the believer shall have a body like the post-resurrection body of Jesus (see Phil. 3:21). Nevertheless, the appearing of Jesus to those anxious disciples was a mighty miracle.

The Manner Of His Appearing

Having considered the moment and the miracle of His appearing, let us think next about the manner of His appearing. Although Jesus entered the room to bring assurance and encouragement to the fearful disciples, the sudden manifestation of His presence multiplied their fright. Luke says the disciples were "terrified" (Lk. 24:37). There are times when the only thing more terrifying than having Christ at some distance is to have Him enter into your presence.

But, Jesus, the meek and lowly Nazarene, the gentle Lamb of God, the Lord of love, always the ministering One, calmed the disciples' fear by saying, "Peace be unto you." This was the genuine positional peace with God that Jesus had promised the disciples in John 14:27. This was the peace which He had made possible through "the blood of His cross" (Col. 1:20).

Obviously, Jesus could have chided the disciples for their cowardice. He could have rebuked them for their lack of faith. He could have upbraided them for their faltering commitment. He could have condemned Peter for his denial. Quite to the contrary, however, having put away their sins, He was now only interested in banishing their fears and anxieties. This caring, loving spirit characterized the manner of His appearing.

The Action Of Jesus

Having spoken peace to the hearts of the disciples, Jesus went into action by showing them His nailed-pierced hands and the wound in His side. Someone asked, "Does the glorified, resurrected body of Christ bear the marks of His wounds at the crucifixion?"

The answer must be a resounding, "Yes!" In Revelation, when the search was being made in heaven to find the one who was worthy to take the scroll and break the seals of judgment, one of the elders found a Lamb exhibiting the marks of sacrifice. This Lamb represents the Son of God who died to take away the sins of the world. The wounds and the nail prints were still there. In fact, those scars may well be the only man-made thing in heaven.

Somehow I feel certain that our glorified bodies will not be scarred or blemished in any way. However, the scars on the body of Jesus will be the emblems of His love and sacrifice for us. His body was marred and scarred for us so that we might be presented to Him without spot or wrinkle or any such thing (see Eph. 5:27). One day the scars, which Jesus bears in His own body, will bring Israel to repentance (see Zech. 12:10). One day those scars will condemn all those who are the enemies of the cross of Christ. One day those scars will be the sure identifying mark to every believer that Jesus Christ is the true Messiah and the Savior of all who believe.

How beautiful are the words of the hymn, "My Savior First of All" by Fannie Crosby:

"When my life's word is ended,
and I cross the swelling tide,
When the bright and glorious morning I shall see;
I shall know my Redeemer when I reach the other side,
And His smile will be the first to welcome me.
I shall know Him, I shall know Him,
And redeemed by His side I shall stand,
I shall know Him, I shall know Him,
By the print of the nails in His hands."

The Ecstasy It Provided

On the night He appeared to the disciples, Jesus revealed Himself, and oh, the ecstasy it provided. When they were finally convinced of the identity and the reality of the risen Lord, they were filled with joy. John exclaimed, "Then were the disciples glad when they saw the Lord" (Jn. 20:20)

Please note that their circumstances had not changed. They were still shut in for fear of the Jews. However, the presence of Christ was like a ray of sunshine piercing through a sky of dark, foreboding clouds. The glory of His presence had ended their suspense, dispelled their fears, removed their doubts, and raised them above their circumstances. Their hearts were filled with immeasurable joy. The resurrection had changed their sunsets into sunrises. It quickened their spirits, ignited their glee, and put the song of victory in their hearts.

The Evidence It Produced

The disclosure of Jesus to the disciples is not only important because of the ecstasy it provided, but also because of the evidence it produced. These disciples gave a firsthand, full-blown, direct, undiluted testimony of their experience with the risen Lord. Approximately sixty years later, when the apostle John wrote his first epistle, he was still under the spell of what happened on the evening of the day Jesus arose from the grave. Consider John's testimony: "That which was from the beginning, which we have heard, which we have seen with our eyes, which we have looked upon, and our hands have handled, of the Word of life; (for the life was manifested, and we have seen it, and bear witness, and show unto you that eternal life, which was with the Father, and was manifested unto us;) that which we have seen and heard declare we unto you, that ye also may have fellowship with us: and truly our fellowship is with the Father, and with His Son Jesus Christ. And these things write we unto you, that your joy may be full" (1 Jn. 1:1-4).

You see, the action of Jesus in disclosing Himself to the disciples is notable because of the ecstasy it provided and the evidence it produced. These disciples were not depending upon some second hand experience to motivate them to change the world. They had seen the risen Lord. They were so personally convinced by the evidence, which they had seen of the resurrection of Christ, that they were perfectly willing to risk their lives for what they knew to be an irrefutable, undeniable truth.

The Assignment Of Jesus

The Mission Of The Savior

In verse 21 of our text Jesus once again bestowed peace upon the disciples. He knew that these disciples needed not only "peace with God" provided by His atoning death, but they needed the "peace of God" in order to launch out with the Gospel into a hostile world void of peace. So, here Jesus assured his disciples of "the peace of God which passeth all understanding" (Phil. 4:7). This is the kind of peace that makes the servant's yoke easy and burden light (see Matt. 11:28-30).

Then Jesus reminded the disciples of the assignment which He Himself had received and fulfilled. He referred to the fact that He had been sent by the Father. Jesus has been sent into the world on a divine mission. He had said, "My meat is to do the will of Him that sent me, and to finish His work" (Jn. 4:34). Our Lord also remarked, "...I seek not mine own will, but the will of the Father which hath sent me... for the works which the Father hath given me to finish.... bear witness of me, that the father hath sent me" (Jn. 5:30, 36).

In His high priestly prayer, Jesus had spoken to His heavenly Father and said, "I have glorified thee on the earth: I have finished the work which thou gavest me to do" (Jn. 17:4). From the cross Jesus cried out, "It is finished" (Jn. 19:30). Jesus did precisely and wholeheartedly what God, the Father, sent Him into this world to do. The apostle Paul said that Jesus was completely conformed to the divine mission, which God had designed for Him and was "obedient unto death, even the death of the cross" (Phil. 2:8).

The Mission Of The Saints

Standing in his glorified body, Jesus commissioned the disciples to carry the Gospel to the world. He told them, "As my Father hath sent me, even so send I you" (Jn. 20:21). This is our divine mandate as well. We are to be on the go with the Gospel. Remember Christ perfectly and completely fulfilled the assignment God gave him. The Bible tells us that Jesus has been given to us as an example that we should follow in His steps (see 1 Pet. 2:21). How well are we following in the steps of Christ? How faithfully are we fulfilling our mission on this earth?

Too often the church is like a football team that practices for a game that is never played. Can you imagine a college football team or a professional football team practicing, as surely they must, and yet never planning to play another game? Such football practice sessions are grueling, risky, bone crushing, and exhausting. Playing college or professional football requires constant, year-round, never-ending conditioning and stringent discipline. The running, the weight lifting, the skull sessions, the physical strength, the mental toughness, and the emotional preparedness--it's unbelievable! Can you imagine an athlete going through all that with no plans to play again? It's unthinkable!

Yet, there are people who go to church (the practice sessions) for years who never attempt to play in the game (spreading the Gospel). We are failing to fulfill our commission. Our Lord has specified us as the "sent out ones," yet many have not responded to the divine charge. So often Christians are like a whole lot of people with colds--all sitting around sneezing at each other, but nobody catches it because everybody's got it. We must move beyond the walls of the church to where the people are and tell them of Jesus and that "there is none other name under heaven given among men whereby we must be saved" (Acts 4:12).

I heard about a certain Bible society that was in a serious debate over the kind of cover that they would use on a new translation of the Word of God. One of the members of the society insisted that a cheap cover be used so that the copy would be inexpensive and thus accessible to many people. Another member insisted that they use an expensive binding since the Bible is the Word of God and deserves the very best. A third member suggested that they bind the new edition in "shoe leather." Amen! That is exactly the kind of binding that the Word of God needs. Every born again believer should be busy projecting the message of the Bible to a lost and dying world. We are to go out into the highways and hedges and compel them to come in. The primary purpose of evangelism is to get the church out of the church. It is so easy to hide in what we have come to call our "sanctuaries" and sing our hymns and hear the sermon and simply forget that a world without God and without hope is eternally lost. Let us bind the Gospel in shoe leather and go where the people are.

The Appropriation Of Jesus

Jesus never issues commands or makes assignments without providing the resources necessary to fulfill those commands. So, having commissioned His disciples in verse 21, He equipped them with power in verse 22. Our text tells us that Jesus breathed on His disciples and said, "Receive ye the Holy Ghost." This is Christ's holy exhalation. The Greek work translated "breathe" is used only here in the New Testament. However, when the first Jewish scholars translated the Hebrew Scriptures into the Greek language, a work known as the Septuagint, this is the Greek word they used to signify the word "breathed" in Genesis 2:7: "And the Lord God formed man of the dust of the ground, and breathed into his nostrils the breath of life; and man became a living soul." Just as man's original creation was completed by the breath of God, so now the breath of the resurrected Lord made of the disciples a new creation and gave them the power to generate the same spirit in others.

This holy exhalation has provoked some rather interesting discussion. For example, there are those who believe that when Jesus breathed on the disciples, they received the Holy Spirit. Others contend that when Jesus breathed upon these men and said, "Receive ye the Holy Ghost," they were regenerated and baptized by the Holy Spirit into the body of Christ. Yet others have purported to believe that in this experience the disciples received only a gift of the Holy Spirit, or a symbolic expression of the Holy Spirit.

The Pledge Of The Spirit

I believe that when Jesus breathed upon the disciples they received the pledge that the Holy Spirit would come. The text does not indicate in any way that they received the Holy Spirit when Jesus breathed upon them and said, "Receive the Holy Ghost." In fact, in verse 26, we read that the disciples were still in that room with the door shut. Surely they would not still be huddled together in some clandestine gathering place if they had received the Holy

Spirit. Their gathering gives more evidence of being tentative than it does of authority and power. Jesus had said, "But ye shall receive power, after that the Holy Ghost is come upon you: and you shall be witnesses unto me both in Jerusalem, and in all Judea, and in Samaria, and unto the uttermost part of the earth" (Acts 1:8).

Actually, the tense of the verb "receive" lends itself to be translated "begin now to receive the Holy Spirit." Jesus was simply trying to get the disciples to prepare themselves for the power, which the Holy Spirit would bestow upon them on the day of Pentecost. In fact, Jesus told them to tarry in Jerusalem until they were endued with power from on high (see Lk. 24:49). In order to receive His power, they had to be spiritually prepared.

I believe they must have spent those days in that room in Jerusalem repenting of their sins and selfishness, getting in unity with one another, and getting their hearts right. Jesus had breathed on them, giving them a foretaste or a pledge that the Holy Spirit would surely come and thus motivating them to get ready for the advent of His coming. When the Spirit came, in Acts 2, the disciples were ready and the miracle of Pentecost occurred.

The Presence Of The Spirit

Today, every believer in Jesus has the Holy Spirit. To the Roman believers Paul wrote, "Now if any man have not the spirit of Christ, he is none of His" (Rom. 8:9). The problem we have today is that we have at our disposal post-Pentecostal power, but we live pre-Pentecostal lives. We've gotten stuck somewhere between Calvary and Pentecost. We are huddled in our gathering places and seem to have forgotten that Christ has not only breathed on us and given us the pledge of the Spirit, but He has also blessed us and given us the power of the Spirit.

We have not been given keys that might work, like the "Let's Make a Deal" keys; we have been given *the* key, even the presence of the indwelling Holy Spirit that right now can clothe us with witnessing power and grace. We must, however, be submissive to His power if we are to be used by Him.

In the concluding verse of our text, Jesus says, "Whosoever sins you remit, they are remitted unto them; and whosoever sins ye retain, they are retained" (v. 23).

Now, this sounds as if we have the arbitrary right to forgive sin. Does this passage say that the church has the right to grant absolution? Is that the implication of Jesus? Absolutely not! Only God has the authority to forgive sin. The Lord God has said, "I, even I, am he that blotteth out thy transgressions for mine own sake, and will not remember thy sins" (Is. 43:25). Mark 2:7 specifies that only God can forgive sins.

The Pronouncement Of The Spirit

What Jesus is doing here is conferring upon spirit filled disciples the authority of declaring whose sins are forgiven and whose sins are unforgiven. Do we have that right and authority today? Yes! If one has not repented of his sins and turned to Christ in faith, we have the right, in the power of the Holy Spirit, to declare that his sins are unforgiven. If one has confessed his sins, repented, and trusted the redeeming work of Christ for salvation, we have the authority to pronounce him as cleansed and forgiven.

One of the great joys that I have as a Christian is the joy of leading people to faith in Christ and kneeling down and praying with them as they invite Jesus to come into their hearts. God has given me the right to say to them, "Welcome to God's family. You are a child of God. Your sins are forgiven. The Holy Spirit has come to take up residence in your heart. Your name is written down in the Lamb's Book of Life. You have a home in heaven. This is going to be the first day of the best of your life." God has given us the privilege and authority to say those words to the new convert.

By the same token, we have the privilege and authority to say to the one who refuses to repent and rejects the testimony of the Holy Spirit concerning Christ that his sins are retained. I not only have the right, but I also have the glorious privilege of proclaiming the whole counsel of God. Included in that counsel are the words: "But the fearful, and unbelieving, and the abominable, and murderers, and whoremongers, and sorcerers, and idolaters, and all liars, shall have their part in the lake which burneth with fire and brimstone: which is the second death" (Rev. 21:8). Please notice that according to this verse the first two on the list of the damned are the "fearful" and the "unbelieving." The person who does not believe on the Lord Jesus Christ is unforgiven and is destined for hell. His sins are retained.

You see, Jesus has not only told us what to do and given us the power to do it, but He has also given us the authority to pronounce the truth of God upon both those who are forgiven and those who are dead in trespasses and sins. Furthermore, if we do not preach the Gospel to the people of the world, their sins will not be forgiven. We have the only thing that will bring forgiveness to a lost and dying world. It is the message of redemption in Jesus Christ. The breath of God upon us and in us enables us to proclaim this message with authority and power.

"The Bible is the Book above and beyond all books as a river is beyond a rill in reach, as the sun is beyond a tallow candle in brightness, as a orchard is beyond a twig in fruit bearing, as Niagara is beyond a mud puddle in glory. Of the written Word it is written, "Thy testimonies are wonderful" (Ps. 119: 129). Of the living Word, Jesus, it is written: "His shall be called Wonderful" (Is. 9: 6). Seventy times seven is four hundred and ninety, but that number does not equal all the wonders in the Bible, of the Bible and by the Bible." [15]
—*Robert G. Lee*

Theopneustos - The God-Breathed Word
2 Timothy 3:16-17

Flying in airplanes once provided a fascination and a thrill for me. I was enthralled each time I boarded some sleek, "silver bird" to fly to some distant city. No longer am I enamored with the thought of flying at 35,000 feet above terra firma.

Those occasional reports of airline disasters have dampened my enthusiasm for getting airborne any more than necessity requires. Then, of course, there are periodic reports of bizarre things happening like the commercial airliner that had to land on top of a levee near New Orleans years ago. One commercial carrier had a plane that had a portion of the fuselage ripped off during a flight. Several years ago in a parking lot near the Hartsfield-Jackson Atlanta International Airport, an eight-foot piece of an engine cover was found. Having become dislodged from the plane during take off, it had fallen harmlessly to the ground.

More recently, an airplane left the Atlanta airport for a transcontinental flight to Portland, Oregon only to realize that one of the tires had blown out during take-off. The apparent solution to that problem was flying 160 passengers around Atlanta for three hours to use up the fuel before landing back at the same airport. But, such incidents only cause apprehension and trepidation. When an individual chooses to travel by air and then realizes that his selected means of conveyance has been assembled with thousands of parts all put together by the lowest bidder his anxieties are justified.

Recently, when I flew into the Dallas/Fort Worth airport, the plane hit the runway, bounced back into the air, and then touched down for the landing. The flight attendant calmly said, "Welcome to the Dallas/Fort Worth area where you get two landings for the price of one." Most people chuckled; some sighed with relief. I was dealing with tachycardia, byspnea, and paresthesia because of a panic disorder marked by an obvious dystychiphobia (note: ministerial embellishment for emphasis).

Once, a former church member boarded a plane, placed his attaché case in the overhead compartment, sat down and waited for the flight to begin. The flight attendant gave her usual speech: "Fasten your seatbelts and move your trays to an upright and locked position." Suddenly there was a knock at the door of the plane. The door was unlocked and opened. It was the pilot. Those who fly very often probably have both their humorous stories and their horror stories to relate.

Therefore, before I fly, I try to look out the window in the terminal (that's a rather frightening word in itself) to check the sturdiness of the aircraft. When I enter the airplane, I always look in the cockpit and try to at least greet the pilot. I am always comforted when I can determine that his eyes are clear and his speech is not slurred. I am always hopeful that a U. S. Marshall is onboard my flight. Paranoia? Probably, but I just want to commit my life to something that is completely trustworthy. Trustworthiness, reliability and authenticity are precisely what we have in the Bible, the Word of God. As we look at our text, there are several things that I want us to consider.

The Provision Of Holy Scripture

Our text indicates that "all scripture is given by inspiration of God." God Himself is the One who has provided the Holy Scriptures. The phrase "inspiration of God" is a translation of the Greek word "theopneustos." "Theopneustos" is used only here in the New Testament and comes from the Greek words for "God" and "breath." The breath of God, therefore, provides the Holy Scripture. It is God-breathed.

The word "inspiration" does not mean that God breathed into the Scriptures, but that God breathed the Scriptures out. When a person is speaking, his breath passes over his larynx, vocal chords, tongue, the cavity of the mouth, the lips and forms the words. The product of this process is the words that are spoken. The Holy Scripture is the Word of God, the breath of God. In essence, the Bible is the out-breathing of God. Interestingly, a myriad of views exist concerning the inspiration of Scripture. For example, there are those who believe that the Bible is inspired in the same way the great literature of the ages is inspired. This view contends that the Holy Scriptures were produced by man's own intuitive genius.

This is what some have called the rational theory of inspiration, because essentially it denies the supernatural. It offers a rational human explanation for the provision of Holy Scripture.

Those who embrace this theory classify the Bible along with the works of John Milton, Alfred Lord Tennyson, John Bunyan, and Robert Browning. Incidentally, I have heard songwriters claim divine inspiration for their music and preachers who have claimed that their sermons were divinely inspired. Surely, God is offended by some of these claims. There are few things worse than discordant, ill-conceived songs and poorly devised sermons that are accredited to God. But, the God-breathed Holy Scriptures are uniquely inspired and marked by an infallibility that characterizes no other words in human speech.

Then there are those who insist that God gave the general thought and that the writers of the Bible put down the thought and expounded upon it. This "thought theory" of inspiration, for example, would suggest that God prompted Paul to write a treatise on love and that the apostle simply took the thought, the suggestion, and produced 1 Corinthians 13. Those who hold to this theory would contend that God suggested to Solomon the need for an essay on the marital relationship, and that Solomon took the thought and penned the Song of Solomon. They would likewise have us to believe that the apostle, John, was prompted by a divine hint to write a preview of the future and thus express his eschatological contemplations in the Book of the Revelation.

Some churchmen believe that the Bible contains the Word of God, but that inspiration cannot be claimed for every word. This view could be classified as partial inspiration. This view would claim inspiration for the Sermon on the Mount, but not the narrative concerning Jonah and the whale. They would say that the passages offering comfort and encouragement are inspired, but that the sections pertaining to God's wrath and judgment are not. The theory of partial inspiration creates a serious problem because if you believe that the Bible is inspired only in spots, then you must also believe that someone must be inspired to spot the spots.

Another view, closely kin to the theory of partial inspiration, is the contention held by some that the New Testament is inspired, but that the Old Testament is not. Another similar opinion has been described as "progressive revelation." Those committed to this view believe that only the words spoken by Jesus are reliable and trustworthy.

While in seminary I encountered those who taught that the Bible is a book of religion and that no one should expect it to be accurate in the areas of astronomy, geography, geology, history, or natural science. Those who so restrict the reliability and the authority of the Bible remind me of a comment attributed to W. C. Fields of Hollywood fame. A friend once caught Fields reading a Bible during a period of illness and expressed stunned surprise. Fields quickly diminished his friend's concern about any sudden burst of piety by exclaiming, "I'm only looking for loopholes." However, my testimony is that I have studied the Bible for many years; and in the course of my study, I have not found hidden flaws, but have found hidden beauty and consistent truth.

My personal conviction is that of plenary, verbal, dynamic, supernatural inspiration. First of all, there is a dynamic, supernatural element about the Holy Scriptures. Please remember that God does practically everything by His breath. In Psalm 33:6, the Bible declares, "By the Word of the Lord were the heavens made: And all the hosts of them by the breath of His mouth." God breathed the universe into existence. Furthermore, He breathed man into existence. He "formed man of the dust of the ground, and breathed into his nostrils the breath of life: and man became a living soul" (Gen. 2:7). Similarly, He breathed the Scriptures into existence.

At the Southern Baptist Convention in St. Louis, Missouri, in 1987, Dr. Jerry Vines preached a message entitled, "A Baptist and His Bible." In that message Dr. Vines said, "In inspiration, God picked up the lifeless pages of man's composition and the Bible became a living Book. Hebrews 4:12 (RSV) says, 'For the Word of God is living.' This Book pulsates with life. It breathes, bleeds, sings, and weeps. Charles H. Spurgeon said, 'If you cut this book into a thousand pieces, every part would grow and live.' Just as a little child puts a sea shell to its ear and can hear the blowing of the waves in the sea, so we with childlike faith hear the breath of God blowing through the pages of the Bible."[16]

Peter, in writing of the inspiration of the Bible, states: "For the prophecy came not in old time by the will of man: but holy men of God spake as they were moved by the Holy Ghost" (2 Pet. 1:21). The phrase "moved by the Holy Ghost" is a delightful figure of speech. In the original language the idea of a sailing vessel is portrayed. Occasionally, the "tall ships" will gather along some populated harbor to display their stately sails. The wind gets into those great sails and the ship moves forth in majestic grandeur. In like fashion these holy men of God were borne along by the wind or breath of God and used to write His Word in majestic grandeur.

God breathes upon man and produces through the dynamic and style of that human personality His own inspired, infallible Word.

So, the Word of God is dynamic, supernatural, alive, and powerful; I also believe in the plenary inspiration of the Bible. The word "plenary" means "complete in every part." When the United States Congress meets in plenary session such as when the President gives the State of the Union Address, every member of both the Senate and the House of Representatives is expected to be there. It is an all-inclusive gathering of all members of both Houses.

The word "all" in 2 Timothy 3:16, comes from the Greek word "pasa" and can also be translated "every." Therefore, all Scripture and every Scripture are inspired. Dr. Hershel Hobbs said that the word "pasa" means, "that every single part of the whole is God-breathed." In other words, Genesis 1:1, is inspired in the same way as John 3:16. Furthermore, we can claim inspiration for Revelation 22:21, just as much as we can for Psalm 23. It is all inspired and awe inspiring.

The late Dr. Adrian Rogers told about a rather brash, but sincere, young preacher who was proclaiming the glorious Gospel on a busy street corner in a large eastern city. As he proclaimed the truth of God, he had to contend with several hecklers who were trying to disrupt his train of thought. Finally, one of the dissidents walked right up in the face of the preacher and said, "I don't believe one word you are saying. Furthermore, I don't believe the Bible. And, besides that, I challenge you to prove one verse out of the Bible."

So, with that challenge the preacher grabbed the man's nose with his thumb and forefinger and twisted it until the blood poured profusely from his nostrils. Then, the preacher turned in his Bible to Proverbs 30:33, and read, "Surely the churning of milk bringeth forth butter, and the wringing of the nose bringeth forth blood...."

Plenary inspiration means that all of the Bible is inspired - every part, every section, every chapter, every verse - the books of history as well as the gospels, the books of poetry as well as the epistles of Paul, and the books of law as well as the apocalypse.

Furthermore, I believe in the verbal inspiration of the Bible. "Verbal" inspiration means "word inspiration" from the Latin term for word. The Bible consists of words and if there is divine inspiration, it must include "verbal inspiration." Therefore, in the Bible the Spirit of God so superintended the writing process that we have recorded in Holy Scripture the Word of God in the language of men. The Bible, therefore, does not really give an account of men's religious experiences, but rather the very words of God.

Hear the words of David, the sweet Psalmist of Israel, in 2 Samuel 23:2: "The Spirit of the Lord spoke by me and His word was in my tongue." The Holy Spirit actually used David's tongue to communicate God's words. Similarly, God so formed the life and the personality of the other writers of Holy Scriptures that they wrote down the very words of God.

I love words and the study of the derivation of words, linguistics and etymology. It is thrilling to me to think that every word of Holy Scripture is divinely inspired and of great significance. Realizing the importance of words, men have spent their lives studying

Hebrew and Greek, burning the midnight oil in the declination of nouns and the conjugation of verbs, to ferret out the absolute truth of the sacred writings. Every word tingles with meaning and weighs a ton. There is not to be a word added to or subtracted from the Holy Scriptures (Deut. 4:2 and Rev. 22:18-19). Indeed, God is intent on preserving every jot and tittle of His Word (Matt. 5:17-18). The word "jot" refers to the ninth letter of the Greek alphabet and is akin to the Hebrew "yodh" which is similar to a comma in appearance and is the smallest letter in the Hebrew alphabet. The "tittle" is a reference to "keraia" which is a diminutive appendage that appears on several Hebrew letters that is about 1/32 of an inch long. Jesus was not only interested in the significance and the preservation of each word, but did not want even a "yodh" or "keraia" to pass away.

To me one cannot deny or discredit one word without discrediting the entire body of Scripture. To attempt to diminish or depreciate one word of Scripture would be as foolish as the actions of a certain man who had been admitted to an institution to regain his mental equilibrium. One day a visitor saw this man using a sledgehammer on the foundation of the dormitory. He had already managed to chip away a piece of the corner of the foundation. The visitor tactfully asked the inmate with the sledge hammer, "What are you doing?"

The man stopped his working, leaned against his instrument of destruction, and said, "Well, can't you see? I am knocking away the foundation of this building."

The visitor replied, "I do see that, but don't you live in this building?"

With that, the man picked up his sledgehammer and said, "of course I do, but I live upstairs."

To discredit the Word of God is to give evidence of extreme foolishness. In the Holy Scriptures we have a reliable, trustworthy, sure foundation provided by God upon which to rest our faith and our future.

The Profitability Of Holy Scripture

Since the Bible is a product of divine inspiration, it is an extremely profitable book. In the economy of God it could not be otherwise, for He has a plan and a purpose for every provision. The provision of God's Word is profitable first for "doctrine." The Bible is God's reservoir of truth from whence we can learn eternal and spiritual realities. To the Roman Christians Paul wrote, "For whatsoever things were written aforetime were written for our learning, that we through patience and comfort of the Scriptures might have hope" (Rom. 15:4).

The Bible, for example, teaches us all we need to know about the doctrine of soteriology or salvation. In writing to Timothy, Paul declared, "And that from a child thou hast known the Holy Scriptures, which are able to make thee wise unto salvation through faith which is in Christ Jesus" (2 Tim. 3:15). Near the conclusion of his gospel the apostle John avowed, "But these are written, that you might believe that Jesus is the Christ, the Son of God; and believing ye might have life through His name" (Jn. 20:31). Furthermore, we know that "faith cometh by hearing, and hearing by the Word of God" (Rom. 10:17).

Actually, the Word of God is not only profitable to communicate the doctrine of salvation, but it also contains the statement and the standard for every doctrine in the Christian faith. Any message you hear, any vision you see, and any spiritual experience that you encounter must conform to the truth of Holy Scripture. The Bible must be that standard by which all experiences are validated and all truth is affirmed.

The Holy Scriptures are also profitable for "reproof." This simply means that the Word of God is the Holy Spirit's instrument of conviction. It exposes all that is unholy and false in our lives. In Hebrews we are told that the Word of God "is a discerner of the thoughts and intents of the heart" (Heb. 4:12). The Greek word for "discerner" is "kritikos," from which we get our word "critic." The Word of God is profitable for "reproof" because it shows us up for what we really are. It is even a critic or a discerner of the thoughts of the hearts of men.

I was reading in Proverbs recently and came across the verse: "All the ways of a man are clean in his own eyes; but the Lord weigheth the spirits" (Prov. 16:2). I must confess that when I read that verse I got under deep conviction. That verse described me. So often I look at my life and my place in the church and in society and I feel good about myself, clean in my own eyes. Then, I began to realize that my goodness is determined not by me, but by how I measure up on God's scales. The real conviction came when I realized that

God not only weighs my deeds, but my motives and my spirit. The reminder that God knows the intent of the heart and the inclinations of the innermost spirit can sometimes be very disturbing. I got on my knees and asked God to give me high and holy motivations and to renew a right spirit within me.

Again, our passage in 2 Timothy shows us that the Holy Scripture is profitable for "correction." This means that the Word of God is effective in restoring the fallen saint to an upright position and setting his feet on a right path.

I had the privilege of preaching a revival for Dr. Terry Williams when he was pastor of Central Baptist Church in Corbin, Kentucky. As a young man Terry was working on an oilrig 150 miles off the shore in the Gulf of Mexico. Terry spent much of the spring of 1979 fighting the call of God into the pastoral ministry. The Lord was dealing with him. He purposely would leave his Bible at home when he went to the oilrig because he did not want God dealing with him. However, on June 1, 1979, Terry Williams knelt beside his bunk and prayed, "Dear God, if you want me to preach, give me a sign this week."

On the very next day a layman representing Gideon's International flew out to the oilrig on a helicopter for the purpose of distributing Bibles to the workmen. Terry interpreted the visit of this Gideon as an answer to prayer, but he continued to look for further confirmation from God. He prayed that God would reveal His will. Terry Williams opened his Bible and the first passage that he read was Mark 6:7-13, which begins with the words, "And He called unto Him the twelve and began to send them forth by two and two; and gave them power over unclean spirits." In verse 12, the Bible declares that "...they went out, and preached that men should repent."

Terry was not yet fully convinced that God was calling him into the ministry, and so he asked for God to give him added confirmation. This time he took the Bible and perchance opened it to Romans 10:14-15, where the question is asked, "And how shall they hear without a preacher?" With only a remnant of rebellion left in his heart, Terry Williams said, "Lord, if you will give me one more passage of Scripture to assure me that it is your will for me to be a preacher of the Gospel, then I will submit to whatever you want me to do." This time he opened the Bible to John 21, and the first words that he read were the words of Jesus to Simon, "Feed my sheep."

The Word of God had provided the "correction" that Terry Williams needed. He began to think in terms of preparing himself educationally and spiritually for a pastoral ministry. Since that time God has used him in a significant way to touch many lives for the cause of Christ.

Notice also that the sacred writings are profitable "for instruction in righteousness." This simply means that the Bible will be profitable in helping the believer to be trained, educated, and disciplined in righteousness.

Several years ago in the Eastside Baptist Church in Marietta, Georgia, our young people were challenged to participate in a program of Scripture memorization. After several months those who had participated in the process of memorizing Scripture began to share testimonies of how God was giving them victory in their walk with Christ. They were finding unusual power to resist temptations. They were being given boldness to share their faith with their peers. They sensed that they were growing in their relationship to Christ and their unusual spiritual maturity was becoming apparent to others. The Psalmist said, "Thy word have I hid in mine heart that I might not sin against thee."

The apostle Peter said, "According as His divine power hath given unto us all things that pertain unto life and godliness, through the knowledge of Him that hath called us to glory and virtue" (2 Pet. 1:3). Please notice that the things that pertain to life and godliness come through knowledge of Him. The knowledge of Him comes about as a result of dwelling richly in the Word of God. So, we discover that the sacred writings are profitable "for instruction in righteousness."

The Permanency Of The Holy Scriptures

The Word of God never grows old. While it is a book of antiquity, it is as current and as up-to-date as tomorrow's newspaper. It has about it the mark of timelessness.

When I was in the fourth grade, my teacher was Lila Belle Cox. She was a large, intimidating woman and a strict disciplinarian who prided herself in teaching her pupils to master the art of handwriting. I had great difficulty in making a capital "G" that suited her standard of excellence. Miss Cox called me in front of the class one day, wrote an impeccable "G" on the chalkboard, and told me to copy her example. With painstaking effort, I wrote on that chalkboard until I had satisfactorily emulated her example. My "G" became a rather amazing facsimile of her perfect specimen, if I do say so.

Psalm 119:89 declares, "Forever, O Lord, thy word is settled in heaven." The word "settled" means "established, set up," like concrete when it is set. Such concrete is established and cannot be changed. Our Bibles today are copies of that perfect, fixed, and timeless Word of God in the heavens. It was there in the beginning. It shall be there world without end. The Holy Scriptures can be trusted yesterday, today, and forever. Isaiah declared, "The grass withereth and the flower fadeth: but the word of our God shall stand forever" (Is. 40:8). What a splendid affirmation of the permanency of God's Word! Regardless of the shifting sands of time and the ever changing circumstances of life, the Word of God is steadfast and sure.

In contrast to the eternality of the Word of God, some of my college textbooks are now practically obsolete. The onrush of scientific information has made a ten-year-old book of science passé. When I was in elementary school, there were only ninety-four known elements in the earth. Now, scientific research has concluded that there are well over 110 elements comprising this world in which we live. My college science textbooks predated the microchip, the laser, the silicone chip, the pacemaker for the heart, and even the pocket calculator.

There are constant changes and discoveries in the field of medicine, astronomy, physics, chemistry, communications, and transportation. The Bible, however, is the old time, new time, all time, forever-current Word of God. Jesus declared, "Heaven and earth shall pass away, but my Word shall not pass away" (Matt. 24:35). Later the apostle Peter admonished his readers, "Being born again not of corruptible seed but of incorruptible by the Word of God which liveth and abideth forever" (1 Pet. 1:23).

The Bible is not the book of the month or the book of the year; it is the book of the ages. It has outlived, outranked, and outreached all other books put together. It not only transcends all other books in its permanency, but also in its power. There is just an amazing difference between the books that men make and the Book that makes men.

The Product Of Holy Scripture

The product of the Holy Scripture is a mature Christian who is complete and permanently equipped to live a life that pleases God and do the work God wants him to do. "All Scripture is given by inspiration of God...that the man of God may be perfect, thoroughly furnished unto all good works" (2 Tim. 3:16) Before his death, I had the privilege of spending some time with evangelist Jess Hendley. He was in his mid-eighties at the time. He was well versed in both the Hebrew and the Greek Scriptures. He had been studying the Bible for over 60 years. He veritably lived in the Word of God. He glowed with a supernatural radiance and absolutely lived to feast on the riches of God's Word. He found it to be a "lamp unto (his) feet and a light unto (his) path" (Ps. 119:105). Brother Jess told me that when he was a child his parents gave him *Hurlbut's Stories of the Bible.* He said, "I devoured that book. While other boys were out playing games, I was inside reading the pages of that book."

At twelve years of age, Jess Hendley joined the church, but when he was twenty his mother died, and he realized his lost condition. He began reading about the Lord's return in Revelation 19, and in the process of reading that passage of Scripture, he was saved and described his conversion as a "Pauline experience." He lived in the glory of that experience for six months and began immediately to study the Bible intensely. Shortly after his conversion, he was called to preach.

The great old saint of God once said, "We know the greatness of God from creation, but we can only know the heart of God through His Word. Words convey thoughts, and when I am studying the Word of God I feel that my mind is in touch with the mind of God. I am consumed with the desire to know Him. I have a passion and a hunger to know His Word. My greatest desire is to get lost in God."

I asked Brother Jess, "How much time do you spend each day studying the Word of God?"

He said, "It would be far easier for me to tell you the amount of time that I spend apart from the Word of God. I am more hungry for its truths today than ever." Jess Hendley was completely and permanently equipped to live a life that pleased God and to do the work that God wanted him to do. He was a vessel fit for the Master's use.

Dr. Adrian Rogers, who was pastor of the Bellevue Baptist Church in Memphis, Tennessee and one of the greatest men of God in Southern Baptist life, said that the greatest enemy of the Bible is not the liberal or the cultist or the humanist or the atheist, but the "so-called Bible believer" who doesn't read it and who doesn't love it and live by it. Let us make our commitment to live in the Word of God, so that the power of God may rest upon our lives.

Here are eight clues indicating that a church is dead:

1. Have lost their sense of mission to those who have not heard about Jesus Christ and do not pant after the Great Commission   2. Exist primarily to provide fellowship for the "members of the club"   3. Expect their pastors to focus primarily on ministering to the members' personal spiritual needs   4. Design ministry to meet the needs of their members   5. Have no idea about the needs of the "stranger outside the gates"   6. Are focused more on the past than the future   7. Often experience major forms of conflict   8. And watch the bottom line of the financial statement more than the number of professions of faith [17]

—*Bill Easum*

A Boneyard + A Breath = A Battalion
Ezekiel 37:1-14

To ever experience a genuine life changing, spiritual revival would be difficult for the average suburban church-going American family. The American family of the 21st century is maxed out commitment wise. Every ounce of energy, every moment of time, every dollar of income, and every modicum of ability is basically committed to the hilt.

The typical suburbanite is an industrious person. Many suburban Americans leave home at six o'clock in the morning, drive for an hour to get downtown to work, and come dragging in at six or seven o'clock in the evening. The workload being carried by those engaged by corporate America is tremendously demanding. The philosophy is: "get all you can, can all you get, sit on the lid and poison the rest." 'Work' is the word inscribed upon every rung on the ladder to success.

The work habits of the average American are inspired by a materialistic view of life. The quest for things is becoming a matter of increasing importance. Most folks in our society spend the first half of their lives trying to accumulate "things" and the last half of their lives trying to keep people from taking those "things" away. Even in the Sunday worship experience it is very difficult for the thoroughly modern American to sing, "All to Jesus I surrender, all to Him I freely give."

This earthly-minded perspective has practically eliminated any contemplation of "heaven" anymore in American churches. When is the last time you sang "In the Sweet By and By" or "Beulah Land" or "On Jordan's stormy banks I stand, and cast a wishful eye to Canaan's fair and happy land, where my possessions lie?" Most of us have succeeded in making this pilgrim land down here so comfortable that we do not even think about heaven. We have feathered our nests down here and dismissed any idea about laying up treasures in glory.

Not only are the American people an industrious people and a materialistic people, but they are also a recreational people. I must admit that I enjoy recreational activities as much as the next person, but there seems to be a preoccupation with sports and recreation in our land. Those who do not participate seem to enjoy being spectators.

Several years ago I was making phone calls on a Saturday afternoon to invite some chronic absentees back to church. One lady proceeded to give me a long list of her ailments, which had apparently immobilized her for months and reduced her to a near invalid status. At least that was the impression she gave me on the telephone. That same night I went to see my boys play soft-ball. They needed an umpire to call balls and strikes, and I was conscripted for the job. I put on a baseball cap and assumed my position behind the catcher to call the game. In the second inning I called a boy out on a close play at home plate. All of a sudden I was showered with a barrage of the most uncharitable words you ever heard in your life.

There was a woman in the stands who called me everything but a child of God. Finally, I turned around to find out who was hurl-ing all these venomous epithets in my direction. I discovered that it was the mother of the boy that I had called out at the plate and the woman I had called on the phone that afternoon – the woman who had given me the litany of her ailments. You can imagine how surprised I was to see her in such vigorous, vociferous ani-mation. However, when I turned around and she realized who I was, she became as white as a sheet and apparently lapsed into a catatonic state because I never heard another word out of her the entire evening.

Americans are a mobile people. We have the means and the ability to travel and we choose to travel on the weekend. There is nothing wrong with travel, but it can become an impediment to consis-tency and faithfulness to Christ and the church. Two preachers were discussing this situation in their churches and one claimed that his congregation was just too close to the beach, and on the weekends the people would travel there, affecting their attendance and offerings." The other preacher said, "I'm just as close to the beach as you are but our problem is not that we are too close to the beach: we are just not close enough to the Lord. When we get close enough to the Lord, the beach won't matter."

Suburban America is also religious. Even though religion may be an important part of our lives, there is little evidence that it is more important than any other part. Christians seem to be particularly nominal in their commitment to Biblical standards. In fact, Christianity has become a rather anemic thing in suburban America. Perhaps that is why someone has said that "third world Christianity" has more power and more potential for changing the world than the brand of Christianity found in America today.

We seem to be so possessive of our time, comforts and lifestyles that there is little time for prayer, a waning interest in personal Bible study, and scarcely a passing interest in any kind of spiritual renewal. Are we so locked into who are and what we are that there is no will to change? Is what we are experiencing in the church as good as it is going to get? The truth is that if we have all of God we ever want, we have all of God we will ever get.

Too many churches are content with the status quo, which is marked by a general deadness that is occasionally interrupted by some kind of spiritual shock treatment that produces an occasional convulsive spark of life. I, for one, am not about to be content with anything, which resembles death, especially when God is in the business of reviving the dead with His resuscitating breath. In our text we are going to discover how the breath of God transformed a desolate bone yard into a dynamic battalion of marching men. In Ezekiel 37, the revival of these bones symbolizes the restoration of the Israelites from their captivity. It is also an emblem of the Jew's ultimate return to the land of promise. Furthermore, this text figuratively portrays God's power to enliven the church and surcharge it with the dynamic of the Holy Spirit.

A Descriptive Place

Our text indicates that the prophet Ezekiel was transported by the Lord to an ancient valley of death. Ezekiel's place of divine appointment was neither attractive nor promising, but no one ever had a more definite call. Ezekiel declares, "The hand of the Lord was upon me, and carried me out in the spirit of the Lord, and set me down in the midst of the valley which was full of bones" (Ez. 37:1). "The hand of the Lord" and "the Spirit of the Lord" were operative in the prophet's life. Ezekiel had been directed and delivered to a place of death and desolation by divine mandate. The Lord never promised Ezekiel a life characterized by "no work and all ease, all honey and no bees." When God called Ezekiel, He said, "...son of man, I send thee to the children of Israel, to a rebellious nation...for they are impudent children and stiff hearted. I do send thee unto them: and thou shalt say unto them, thus saith the Lord God" (Ez. 2:3-4). This was Ezekiel's divinely ordained preaching assignment.

Sometimes the preacher will find his congregation as rebellious and unreceptive as Ezekiel did.

When Isaiah exhorted Israel to obey God, they did not receive his message with gladness. In fact, he said to Israel, "...thou art obstinate, and thy neck is as an iron sinew, and thy brow brass" (Is. 48:4). When Stephen defended his faith before the High Priest and the Sanhedrin, he encountered a defiant audience. He said, "Ye stiff necked and uncircumcised in heart and ears, ye do always resist the Holy Ghost..." (Acts 7:51). Dr. Vance Havner said that occasionally he would preach in a church where the look on the faces of the people would curdle milk. I think, however, I would rather preach in a place where there is defiance and resistance than in a place where there is death. I think I had rather preach to a convention of atheists than to a valley of dry bones. Despair is rational and hope is absurd in a situation like the one encountered by Ezekiel.

During my first fulltime pastorate I would to go to the church on Saturday nights, turn on the pulpit lights, and practice preaching my sermon to an empty auditorium. Every Saturday night I followed the same routine. I would wax eloquently before that lumber yard of empty pews. I never expected any response: and I never got any response until one night three mischievous teenagers decided to rock my world. They knew about my Saturday night routine and had arrived at the church ahead of me. They had entered the worship center and were quietly lying down in the pews at the back of the building. I was preaching an animated sermon complete with inflections of the voice, gestures of the hand and pounding the pulpit. At one strategic point I raised my voice for emphasis and those three teenagers sat up in the pews and said "Amen!" That was the last time I ever practiced my sermon in church on Saturday night.

Sometimes you will have a church meeting where there are just a lot of empty pews. Sometimes you will have a church meeting where the pews are just full of a lot of empty people. In either case there is a deadness that prevails. May God forbid that such death ever prevails in your church or mine. May God forever deliver us from being bone yard Baptists. Far too many churches are characterized by the pitiable and repulsive spectacle of bones that have been dried and bleached by years of exposure to worldly compromise and spiritual drought.

Poor Ezekiel! Assignment: the bone yard! That was the descriptive place from whence his message was to be heralded.

The Desperate Predicament

When Ezekiel actually surveyed the situation and saw all the bones, he observed that "there were very many in the open valley" and that "they were very dry" (v. 2). It was a scene of silent desolation. The valley did not contain skeletons, but an indiscriminate mass of bones so thick that the plain was white with the chronic leprosy of death. As we ponder those bleached bones, picked clean by the vultures and scattered about in hopeless confusion, let us think of some of the characteristics of death.

A dead person has no purpose. Try to discover the purpose of a dead man. He is incapable of having goals and dreams and ambitions. A corpse does not establish objectives and execute plans.

A number of years ago the former Olympic champion Bob Richards was visiting a Sunday school class in Long Beach, California. On that particular Sunday he met an overweight grade-school girl wearing thick glasses. She obnoxiously insisted to Richards, "I am going to become a great tennis champion."

The renowned Olympic hero thought the girl's dream was an unrealistic fantasy. However, Billie Jean King had a purpose firmly planted in her heart. Her discipline, persistence, and determination vaulted her into the tennis arena and consequently lifted her into the winner's circle to be the champion she wanted to be.

At fifteen, Mark Spitz declared that he was going to win seven Olympic gold medals. At the 1968 summer games in New Mexico, he won two gold medals. He was sorely disappointed, but he reaffirmed his goal and trained with greater intensity and commitment than ever. Four years later at the 1972 games in Munich, he set seven Olympic records and won seven gold medals, just as he had predicted six years earlier.

Another man, at sixty-five years of age, looked back over his life and saw only a mountain of failures. He had spent much of his career cooking and washing dishes in a little cafe. When he received his first Social Security check for $105, he was so despondent he contemplated suicide. However, instead of taking his life, he mustered up his courage, reviewed his life, and decided to assert himself as a cook. He went to the local bank and borrowed less than one hundred dollars against his next Social Security check. He went to the supermarket and bought some chicken and fried it as only he could do it. This determined retiree then began to go from door to door in Corbin, Kentucky, selling that chicken. That was the beginning of Colonel Sanders' Kentucky Fried Chicken enterprise.

You see, Billie Jean King, Mark Spitz, and Harlan Sanders all had something that the dead do not have. They had a purpose, a goal, and an objective. We must remember that "where there is no vision (purpose), the people perish..." (Prov. 29:18). Examine yourself! Are you spiritually alive? Do you have a divine purpose for your life? Do you have a heavenly vision to direct and motivate your destiny?

Secondly, a dead man has no passion. There is no fire, no zeal, no appetite, no emotion, no heart, and no driving force in the chest cavity of a corpse. A dead man is utterly insensitive to his surroundings. He is moved neither by that which inspires laughter, nor that which prompts grief. Would to God that we had the passion of the apostle Paul who said, "That I may know him, and the power of his resurrection, and the fellowship of his sufferings, being made conformable unto his death" (Phil. 3:10). What is this "fellowship of suffering" that Paul wanted to experience? Actually, there are three kinds of suffering mentioned in the Bible. There is suffering for sin, which is described as punishment. There is also suffering for Christ, which is referred to as persecution. However, there is also suffering with Christ, which is described as passion. It was obviously Paul's desire to share the passion, the heartthrob of the Son of God for a lost and dying world. George McDonald said that Jesus suffered and died, not in order to save us from suffering, but so that our suffering might be like his.

Those who are dead can never enter into this passion, this intense empathy with Christ for a lost world and for a growing church. A corpse cannot rejoice when a prodigal son returns home. A corpse cannot praise God for spiritual victories. A corpse cannot weep when a despairing soul wanders astray. Dead men have no passion. Those who are insensitive to spiritual realities and have a "ho-hum" attitude toward the things of God give more evidence of death than life. Unfortunately, it is evident that many in our churches have spiritual rigor mortis. There is no spiritual purpose or passion in their lives.

Another trait of death is a lack of productivity. People, corporations, and churches that are vibrantly alive are productive. But, death is marked by sterility, stagnation, and barrenness. The church at Sardis was dead. It had a reputation for being alive, but was doubtlessly living only in the afterglow of a glorious past. The altars were empty. The baptistery was covered with cobwebs, and they knew not that the Spirit of the Lord had departed from them (see Rev. 3:1-6). There are churches today with stately buildings, impressive budgets, and endless activities, but the atmosphere in the worship service resembles the mortuary chill of death. They are in the path of the grim reaper's swath, and the stench of their decomposition is already ascending toward the nostrils of God.

One preacher was asked about the health of his church, and replied, "Obviously the folks in my church don't love each other, because I haven't married anybody in the ten years I've been here. They don't love God, because no one ever comes to the altar to make a decision for Christ. I sometimes wonder if God even loves them, because He hasn't seen fit to call any of them home to heaven during the past decade. Otherwise, everything is going well in our church."

There is no purpose, no passion, and no productivity among the dead. The valley of dry bones observed by Ezekiel was a picture of deadness and desolation. It was a desperate predicament. To test Ezekiel's faith, the Lord asked, "Son of man, can these bones live?" (v. 3). The situation looked hopeless! While there is the temptation to write "Mission Impossible" over the desperate predicament we are suddenly reminded of the missing factor – the sovereignty and the omnipotence of God.

So, in response to the Lord's exploratory question, Ezekiel wisely answered, "O, Lord God, thou knowest" (v. 3). Presumption would have responded in the affirmative "yes." Unbelief would have responded with a disconsolate "no." The confident response of faith is forever, "Oh, Lord God, thou knowest." The genuine believer knows, "with men this is impossible; but with God all things are possible" (Matt. 19:26).

A Directed Prophesy

The Lord said to Ezekiel, "Prophecy upon these bones, and say unto them, O, ye dry bones, hear the word of the Lord" (v. 4). Surely, God placed Ezekiel in this most unpromising situation to demonstrate the power of the preached word.

Can't you just imagine the first reaction of Ezekiel? The command to address the constituents of this rather unkempt cemetery is incredible. Ezekiel could have remonstrated with the Lord and said, "You mean that you want me to preach to all these dry, bleached bones? What am I supposed to say? 'Deadly beloved, we are gathered here in the presence of God to join together this ankle bone to this leg bone.'"

To say one word of exhortation or admonition to a valley of bones required great faith. A gallery of saints who had demonstrated a marvelous confidence in God had no doubt encouraged Ezekiel. There was Able who had given evidence of a great faith by offering a more excellent sacrifice than Cain. Noah had demonstrated a remarkable faith by preparing an ark and warning a recalcitrant and unresponsive society of a flood for one hundred and twenty years. Abraham's sojourn to the land of promise was an example of outstanding faith. Moses' choice to suffer affliction with the people of God rather than enjoy the pleasures that abounded in Egypt marked him as a man of faith. Surely the knowledge of these stalwart men of faith motivated Ezekiel to obey the command of God.

This valley of death, however, offers Ezekiel a faith-stretching experience. This scene is full of all kinds of dramatic possibilities. Before this wasteland of disconnected skeletons stands a man to whom has been committed the word of life. Will the "quick and powerful" Word of God make a difference in the midst of death? Is the promise that God's Word shall not return to him void really valid (see Is. 55:11)? Can men be saved, revived, resuscitated by the foolishness of preaching (see 1 Cor.1:21)? Yes, a thousand times yes! When a man of God stands in the power of God to preach the Word of God, many miraculous things become wondrous possibilities.

In a terrible battle a certain army was being soundly defeated. The General called for the bugler and said, "Son, sound the retreat."

The young soldier said, "Sir, I'm sorry, but I do not know how to sound the retreat."

The commander said, "The battlefield is covered with our casualties. Our troops are being defeated. Something must be done to avert further disaster."

The bugler said, "Sir, though I cannot signal a retreat, I can sound forth a charge that will make

dead men rise from the field of battle to march forth to victory."

The faithful preaching of the Word of God will arouse the dead and prepare the people for battle.

A Definitive Promise

God's promise to the dry bones through Ezekiel is recorded in verses 5 and 6: "...behold, I will cause breath to enter into you, and ye shall live: and I will lay sinews upon you, and will bring up flesh upon you, and cover you with skin, and put breath in you, and ye shall live; and ye shall know that I am the Lord." Actually, this prophecy includes God's promise to resurrect the nation of Israel. The status of the nation was deplorable. The distinctiveness of Israel had vanished through compromise. The religious festivals, temple rites, Levitical priesthood, and commitment to the law had virtually disappeared. The dry, disconnected bones now appropriately symbolized their dreadful, shameful condition.

Indeed, the Jews have been "buried" among the nations of the earth as bones scattered over a parched desert. The promise of God is that He will one day gather together the Jews from the ends of the earth and return them to their land. In 1948, with the establishment of the state of Israel, the restoration process was begun. Statistics indicate that already the Jews are filtering back into the land God promised them. The day will come when Israel and Judah will be reunited, for Ezekiel declares: "Neither shall they be divided into kingdoms anymore at all" (Ez. 37:22). The regathering and restoration of the Jews to their land will be completed at the return of Christ. So, the literal definitive promise pertains to Israel's reconciliation to their God and their restoration to their land (see also Jer. 23:7-8; Is. 11:11-12; Ez. 37:14, 25; Ez. 39:28; Amos 9:14-15; Rom. 11:26-27).

These verses not only have a primary application to the Jewish people, but they have a tremendous interpretation for the modern day church. Just as one day God will chasten, cleanse, and restore the Jews by the inbreathing of His Spirit, even so He has the power to cleanse and revive and restore to power His body, the church. Let it be clearly and firmly stated, however, that the restoration of Israel and the revival of the church is possible only through the intervention of God. The church cannot resuscitate herself. To try to enliven and operate a church in the energy of the flesh would be like trying to operate a factory on a flashlight battery. Our efficiency turns out to be deficiency without God's sufficiency. We can agonize, organize, emphasize, and publicize, but we cannot produced a genuine revival. If real renewal comes, it will have to come from God. God can always do more in one service than we can do in a year of service. How wondrous is the power of God! The psalmist declared, "God hath spoken once; twice have I heard this; that power belongeth unto God" (Ps. 62:11).

Dearly beloved, the God who breathed into man's nostrils the breath of life and the Lord Jesus who breathed upon the disciples and said, "Receive ye the Holy Spirit" (Jn. 20:22), is the same God who can breathe upon a bone yard and transform it into a mighty, marching, motivated battalion of believers. To the broken, barren, impotent church, our great God offers a renewed and revitalized life.

A Deliberate Process

A real revival generally is the result of a gradual, deliberate process. For example, there were several stages in the restoration of this "exceeding great army" in Ezekiel 37. The first indication the transformation or "reviving" was about to occur was a "noise." In verse 7, Ezekiel informs us that, "there was a noise." Some scholars interpret this "noise" as the trumpet blast or "the voice of God" which at the end of this age will precede the resurrection of the dead (see 1 Thess. 4:16).

When David wanted to know that moment at which God would have him move his army out against the Philistines, that moment at which God's grace would be poured out to quicken his endeavors, God said, "And let it be, when thou hearest the sound of a going in the tops of the mulberry trees, that then thou shalt bestir thyself" (2 Sam. 5:24). When David heard that noise, he launched his attack to conquer his enemies. The military assault was signaled with a "noise."

In the New Testament, when the kingdom of the Messiah was to be established and the apostles were to beat down the devil's kingdom, they were told not to attempt anything until they received the promise of the Spirit. In Acts 2, we read that the coming of the Spirit was signaled by a noise, a sound. "And suddenly there came a sound from heaven, as of a rushing mighty wind, and it filled all the house where they were sitting" (Acts 2:2).

Listen! Listen! Spiritual renewal starts with a sound. Do you hear anything that hints of revival? Is there a noise on earth that is ascending to heaven? Is there a noise in heaven that is descending to earth?

Next there was "a shaking" to follow the noise in this deliberate process of God. There was a holy commotion! Some have identified this "shaking" as an earthquake. Others have indicated that it must have been something like the vibrations of some peals of thunder accompanying the divine prophecy. Some say the shaking came about as a result of the rustling of bones beginning to come together. Sometimes God introduces some of His mightiest works with a triumphant tremor. Consider Acts 4:31: "And when they had prayed, the place was shaken where they were assembled together;

and they were all filled with the Holy Ghost, and they spoke the Word of God with boldness."

Following the "noise" and the "shaking," "the bones came together, bone to his bone." All the dry, scattered, disconnected bones began to be properly consolidated. This miracle of bones being connected reminds us of the old spiritual, "Dem Bones." In verse 8, we are informed that "the sinews and the flesh came upon them, and the skin covered them above." A deliberate process of assembling and organizing has taken place as these dry bones have become skeletons clothed with flesh and encased in skin. That which started out as a bone yard became a full-fledged mortuary filled with orderly rows of cold, beautiful, compact corpses.

Please observe that the situation was vastly different, but not at all improved, because dead is dead. Some are beautiful when they die; others are ugly. Some die in their youth; others die when they are well stricken with years. Many have been dead for years and their bodies have disintegrated into dust. Some who have recently died appear to have the blush of life still upon their countenance and give the impression of being in a deep sleep. However, every deceased person is marked by decay, decomposition and corruption.

Many churches are not so much symbolized by the valley of dry bones as they are by the assembled skeletons clothed in flesh. The designated hour of worship may be punctiliously proper and yet void of the breath of God. In the "Rhyme of the Ancient Mariner" dead men steered the ship, scrubbed the deck of the ship, hoisted the sails, and rowed the oars. Those seamen were going through all the motions, but they were dead. The church must beware of going through the motions of an external religion that is empty of life and spirit and power.

Having prophesied to the dry bones, Ezekiel then had to prophesy to the wind to breathe on the slain and make them live. The proclamation of mere man had obviously accomplished all that could be accomplished from a human perspective. The dry bones had assembled and been covered with flesh to form a proper appearance. There was a congregation, but not a communion, an assembly, but not an army. The all-pervading breath of God was the one essential missing ingredient.

Actually, "breath" was first mentioned in verse 5 and is obviously the most important element in the process to produce life. Remember that the word "breath" is a translation of the Old Testament word "ruach" which can also be translated "wind" or "spirit." With the breath of life infused into these corpses, they came alive and stood up as an exceeding great army. Jesus said, "It is the spirit (breath) that quickeneth; the flesh profiteth nothing: the words that I speak unto you, they are spirit, and they are life" (Jn. 6:63). The breath (spirit) of God can awaken to newness of life both the dead sinner and the defeated saint.

A Divine Performance

Now instead of a valley of dry bones, there is a living, loyal, united, mighty army. That is precisely what a revival will do—it will make an indifferent, lifeless, lukewarm church into a mighty, militant, marching army.

Both the restoration of Israel and the reviving of the church are a purely divine performance. God said, "And ye shall know that I am the Lord, when I have opened your graves, o my people, and brought you up out of the your graves. And shall put my spirit in you, and ye shall live, and I shall place you in your own land: then shall ye know that I the Lord have spoken it, and performed it, saith the Lord" (Ez. 37:13-14).

Years ago, in the Civil War battle of Kennesaw Mountain, a twenty-year-old Union captain was terribly wounded. He lay bleeding upon the battlefield with his chest "blown open." A medic stopped, saw his condition, bent down to try and detect a heartbeat, and concluded that the young officer was dead. That battlefield marked by heaps of bleeding flesh was another valley of death.

The wounded captain had been left for the night in a pool of blood with no bedding but the ground, no roof but the canopy of heaven, no pitying eyes but the stars, no sound but the call of the nightingale, no companions but his fallen comrades and no hope but the power of prayer.

Back in a New England village the young soldier had a mother and father who were devout Christians. They believed in the power of prayer and had been interceding for their son all through the months of fighting. He went to Yale University and had his faith challenged and destroyed. He became a rebel and was known and registered as an infidel. There were those who would have rejoiced if the battlefield had claimed his life.

That body, however weak and wounded, held on tenaciously to the slightest remnant of life. A myriad of thoughts marched through his brain in dramatic succession that night on the battlefield. The instruction and admonition, which he had received from his godly parents, came back to him. That battlefield suddenly became an altar and that young man was saved by the power of a sovereign God. In the midst of a theater of death God breathed into him the breath of life.

At the breaking of dawn the next morning a platoon of soldiers came to retrieve the dead and found the captain still breathing. They took him to a hospital. As soon as he was able to make a request, he called for a chaplain and told him of his conversion and of his intention to be a committed Christian.

Everyone thought the bleeding soldier had been mortally wounded. The medic had left him for dead. The stretcher-bearer gave him no hope of survival. His comrades thought him to be no longer among the living. However, God, in His grace and power, saw fit to lay His hands upon that boy who had been shredded by shrapnel. Jesus, the One who walked in Galilee, took a stroll through that battlefield that night and entered the heart of a boy whose only hope was in God. That which was accomplished on that field of battle was of God--a divine performance.

By the way, who was that bleeding boy and whatever became of him? He was ordained to the Gospel ministry in 1879. He served as pastor of the Grace Baptist Church in Philadelphia, and later founded the Baptist Temple, developing it into one of the most important churches in America. He started a night school for young preachers, which subsequently became Temple University. This man also founded Samaritan Hospital in 1891. He wrote twenty books, which have been widely read and marvelously influential. Because of the life of this man, Russell Herman Conwell, and his invaluable contribution to America thousands of souls have been saved and many more have been enriched.

The mention of a divine performance speaks of a blessed, beneficial intervention of God. What Russell Conwell did for the cause of Christ and the good of man resulted from the touch of God upon a life that appeared to be no more than a corpse in a field of death. Perhaps you need the touch of God upon your life. Perhaps you need to experience the divine inspiration that occurs when God breathes into you His quickening power. He can enliven you to be a part of a mighty spiritual army. He can quicken you so that you can become a vibrant, vital soldier of the cross.

"The Holy Spirit does not come into the believer's life to fill him, to possess him, to empower him, unless the believer invites Him in. This act of inviting the Spirit into the life and giving Him complete possession of every power of the soul, the will included, is the crowning act of faith. This is not necessary to salvation, but it is necessary to power in service. No one can have the power he needs without this infilling. No one has this fullness of the Spirit as a matter of course. The infilling is received when the believer consciously lays hold of Christ and by faith claims this covenant blessing."[18]

—J. B. Lawrence

A Rushing, Mighty Wind
Acts 2:1-4

In November of 1904 a mighty revival swept through the little principality of Wales. Some years before the Welsh revival, however, a teenager by the name of Evan Roberts heard F. B. Meyer preach on the need of a spiritual awakening. In that service young Roberts made a commitment to pray earnestly for revival. For thirteen years he sought the face of God continually and asked for an outpouring of the Holy Spirit.

Evan Roberts felt the call to preach and began to prepare himself educationally and theologically by enrolling in a preparatory school in New Castle. The burden for revival was so great that he left school and went home to Loughor and found a church where he began to hold prayer meetings for revival. Without any promotion or advertisement, people began coming to make their supplications known to God, asking God for a fresh touch of heaven upon their lives.

As earnest, agonizing cries went up to God from the people night after night the mercy drops of blessing began to fall. Subsequently, a mighty revival swept into the land like a flood tide. The sense of God's presence was overwhelming. The public meetings of worship were marked by a fire and fervor. The spiritual awakening was characterized by the most contrite confessions of sin. The moral climate of the land was lifted noticeably and restitution was being made wherever possible. Sporting events were stricken from the calendar. Political meetings were canceled. A wondrous spirit of liberty marked church meetings. Severed relationships were restored in homes and businesses. Taverns closed their doors because their former patrons had turned to a life of Christianity and sobriety. Houses of ill repute went out of business as the people launched purity crusades. In November and December of 1904 over seventy thousand people were saved as a result of this mighty outpouring of the Holy Spirit.

Another more recent account of the moving of God's Spirit to produce an amazing spiritual harvest is recorded in the book "Thunder in the Valley." This book tells of the missionary service of Doug and Evelyn Knapp, who planted their lives for many years in the remote bush country of Africa's Tanzania. The Kyela district of Tanzania experienced a dramatic spiritual breakthrough between 1978 and 1986, which resulted in nearly thirty-four thousand baptisms. The miraculous spiritual harvest came about as the result of the Knapps' commitment to meet God's conditions for revival. In describing Doug and Evelyn Knapp "Thunder in the Valley" points to "the power of their faith,…their tenacity… (and) their single-minded determination to fulfill their magnificent obsession of winning the district to Jesus Christ." [19]

Most of us never experience revival, and we never see such a spiritual harvest because we have no magnificent obsession and are content to live in the doldrums where the wind of the Spirit seldom blows. The experience of the Knapps in Tanzania simply gives proof to the fact that a strict adherence to the laws of revival result in a mighty moving of the Spirit of God.

Yet another remarkable outpouring of God's Spirit in Africa was experienced in the Moslem dominated country of Kenya in the summer of 1990. Ralph Bethea, a Southern Baptist missionary in Mombasa, along with Dr. Jimmy Draper, then pastor of the First Baptist Church in Euless, Texas, dreamed of a massive evangelistic effort along the Kenya coast. Bethea said, "The Lord promised us if we would be faithful we would see things the prophets yearned to see and we have. We saw what the power of God can do when His people - just ordinary people—pray and make themselves available to Him." During the two-week evangelistic campaign 56,323 professed their faith in Jesus Christ and eighty-four new churches were formed.

The Chicago Tribune recently reported on the revival of Christianity that is changing the religious landscape of China. The article stated, "Christianity – repressed, marginalized and, in many cases, illegal in China for more than half a century is sweeping the country, overflowing churches and posing a sensitive challenge to the officially atheist Communist Party."

There is no reason for the church of the Living Lord to be stuck in neutral when we have the promise of a power that will enable us to live on a supernatural level. Dr. James A. Stewart declared: "As long as the blessed Holy Spirit Himself, the Great Standing

Miracle, abides and works on the earth, the church's potential is the same as it was in the apostolic days." The Pentecostal power was experienced in Wales in 1904, in Tanzania in 1978-1986, in Kenya in 1990 and in China today. But can it be experienced in modern America? Let us look at our text to see if we can discover the principles that produced the revival at Pentecost.

The Meeting Of The Saints

The Apostle Luke is the author of the book of Acts, and in the first verse of chapter two he wrote: "And when the day of Pentecost was fully come, they were all with one accord in one place" (Acts 2:1). Prior to his ascension Jesus had strictly charged the disciples to return to Jerusalem and remain there until they received an infusion of power from heaven (see Lk. 24:49). Jesus did not want the disciples to attempt the divine work without the divine power.

As soon as Jesus was taken up into heaven, Luke records, "Then returned they unto Jerusalem from the Mount called Olivet, which is from Jerusalem a Sabbath day's journey. And when they were come in, they went up into an upper room, where abode both Peter, and James, and John, and Andrew, Philip, and Thomas, Bartholomew, and Matthew, James the son of Alphaeus, and Simon Zelotes, and Judas, the brother of James. These all continued with one accord in prayer and supplication, with the women, and Mary the mother of Jesus, and with His brethren" (Acts 1:12-14). Luke indicates that there were about one hundred and twenty disciples who had gathered in this upper room in a solemn assembly (see Acts 1: 15).

A Special Obedience

First of all, this meeting of the saints was marked by a special obedience. In returning to Jerusalem and waiting for "the promise of the Father," these disciples were giving evidence of their submission to the will of Christ. In the final analysis obedience is the chief requisite to the bestowal of God's richest blessings. There is no substitute for obedience. The Bible declares that "to obey is better than sacrifice, and to hearken than the fat of rams" (1 Sam. 15:22). The Bible also tells us that the Holy Spirit is given to those who obey God (see Acts 5:32). Charles Finney defined revival as "nothing else than a new beginning of obedience to God."

I have memorized and often meditated upon what many have referred to as the Scriptural prescription for revival in 2 Chronicles 7:14. I've given special attention to God's admonition to "seek (His) face." What does that mean? Some time ago the Lord impressed upon my heart the following substitute for that phrase: "Look me in the eyes." I don't know if that will bear much homiletical or exegetical scrutiny, but the idea brought great conviction to my heart. Before we can expect the Lord's richest blessings, we must be able to look Him in the eyes.

When I was a boy I could never look my dad in the eyes when I was being rebellious and disobedient. However, when I was fulfilling my responsibilities around the house, when I was faithfully doing my homework as prescribed by my teacher at school, when I was living in harmony with my brother and sister, when I was following his godly steps and greater wisdom, I could look into his eyes without shame or reproach. An individual will seek the face of God when he is living in obedience, when there is nothing to prevent the "least of His favor."

Today the church is filled with people who know all the spiritual jargon. They perform a multitude of good works and like the rich, young ruler; they have been faithful to keep the Commandments. However, just like that rich, young ruler, they refuse to do the one thing the Lord requests. They lack obedience. Jesus said, "Not every one that saith unto me. Lord, Lord, shall enter into the kingdom of heaven, but he that doeth the will of my Father which is in heaven" (Matt. 7:21). The one hundred and twenty disciples were not just glibly calling Jesus "Lord." In their return to Jerusalem and in their gathering in that upper room, they were "doing the will of God." They were giving evidence of obedience. Before a believer can ever experience God's best, he must come to the place where he is single-minded in his obedience to the Lord Jesus Christ. In his spirit there must be a heartfelt passion to say an everlasting "yes" to the will of God.

A Special Oneness

This meeting of the saints was marked not only by a special obedience, but also by a special oneness. Luke tells us that "these all continued with one accord in prayer and supplication..." (Acts 1:14). Again he informs us that "...they were all with one accord in one place" (Acts 2:1). The Bible obviously places a premium on the saints being in perfect harmony. After the revival at Pentecost, we are informed that the disciples, "continuing daily with one accord in the temple, and breaking of bread from house to house, did eat their meat with gladness and singleness of heart" (Acts 2:46).

To the church in Philippi Paul wrote, "If there be any consolation in Christ, if any comfort of love, if any fellowship of the spirit, if any bowels and mercies, fulfill ye my joy, that ye being like-minded, having the same love, being of one accord, of one mind" (Phil. 2:1-2). Jesus even indicated that a special prayer promise is granted to those who are in agreement and harmony concerning their requests (see Matt. 18:19).

Unfortunately, today it is very difficult for the church to be in harmony and agreement. In the first place, the spirit of unity is impossible in a church when there are husbands and wives in the local assembly with fractured relationships. How can there be oneness in the church when a businessman looks out across the congregation and sees another member who owes him money, and there has been no apparent attempt to reconcile the debt? How can there be fellowship, amity, mutuality, and concord in the church when church members in the same subdivision have been on different sides of a political issue and allowed their differences to breed resentments and bitterness that do nothing but exacerbate the schism?

Two families in the same church lived side by side in a certain neighborhood. One of the families had three boys who loved to play ball. They decided to have a fence built around their property. This project provoked the consternation of the neighbors who scarcely ever needed a reason for being cantankerous. Within a week after the fence was built, those playful boys kicked a football over the fence into the neighbor's front yard. The ill-tempered woman next door confiscated the football and refused to return it to the boys at play. Many attempts were made to try to placate the perturbed neighbors next door, but all attempts failed.

Both of these neighbors went to the same church. Unfortunately, the contentious spirit of the ill-tempered neighbors began to affect the fellowship of the church. When the evangelist came for the spring revival, the church was cold and unreceptive to all efforts to ignite the fires of revival. The pastor told the evangelist about the rift between the neighbors. The evangelist offered to intervene in the conflict. He found the family with the three sons open and receptive and willing to resolve the conflict. But, the couple next door demonstrated an unyielding obstinate spirit. The evangelist learned about the football, which the neighbors were now claiming as their own and asked to see it. Upon viewing the undersized, Nerf football the evangelist began to laugh uproariously.

"What is so funny?" the sneering matron asked.

"Oh, I was just thinking about how foolish you are going to look marching up to the Judgment Seat of Christ or the Great White Throne Judgment with a Nerf football under your arm."

Perhaps the evangelist had a flair for the dramatic, but strife, contention, and discord in the church are serious problems. In fact, the Word declares that God hates those who sow discord among the brethren (see Prov. 6:14, 19). Strife in the church or in a denomination of churches goes against every principle of revival and every promise of God to be found in the Holy Scriptures. Jesus said, "Therefore, if thou bring thy gift to the altar, and there rememberest that thy brother hath ought against thee; leave there thy gift before the altar, and go thy way; first be reconciled to thy brother, and then come and offer thy gift." (Matt. 5:23-24)

Surely that upper room where the disciples gathered was a place of confession, repentance, prayer, reconciliation, and tarrying. Simon the Zealot and Matthew the tax collector got in harmony. The impetuous, boisterous Peter and the mystical, reflective John had their hearts melted together. Doubting Thomas and faith-filled Andrew got on common ground. By the dawning of the day of Pentecost, that upper room in Jerusalem contained one hundred and twenty people whose hearts beat as one.

A Special Occasion

The obedience and oneness of those believers came together on a special occasion—"when the day of the Pentecost was fully come…" (Acts 2:1). The Hebrew name for this religious celebration is "Shavuot" meaning "Weeks." Hence, in the Old Testament it is known as the "Feast of Weeks." The Greek name is "Pentecost" which means "fiftieth" and the day was called that because it occurred fifty days after the Passover Feast. The purpose of this festival was to dedicate the first fruits of the wheat harvest.

In the Old Testament observance of Pentecost, the Jews took the first fruits of wheat, ground it into flour, added oil and leaven, and made two loaves of bread. The loaves were then offered to the Lord along with ten animal sacrifices. This observance occurred on the day after the seventh Sabbath after the Passover, which would have been our Sunday.

The oil used to make the loaves of bread represented the Holy Spirit, which was to be poured out on the day when Pentecost was "fully come." The two loaves symbolized the Jews and the Gentiles who would ultimately comprise the church (some regard the experience in Acts 2 as the Jewish Pentecost and the experience in Acts 10 with the salvation of Cornelius as the Gentile Pentecost). The use of leaven in the bread signified that, though Christ was without sin, the same would never be true of the church. The ten sacrifices (see Lev. 23:18) are emblematic of the perfection and the completion of Christ's atoning and sacrificial death on the cross.

We must remember that the resurrection of Jesus and the outpouring of the Holy Spirit upon the church were events that occurred on Sunday. What better reasons can be found to worship on the first day of the week? The Jewish people have been observing the "Feast of Weeks" for hundreds of years, but all of their previous celebrating had pointed to this ultimate Pentecost when the outpouring of the Holy Spirit upon the church became a reality. Undoubtedly, the events that transpired in Acts 2 prompted Luke to denote this Pentecost as the transcendent one, saying, "And when the day of Pentecost was fully come..." There had been fifteen hundred Pentecosts, but this one was the one in which all the others were fulfilled. This Pentecost was different.

The same thing can be true in our church worship experiences. For years we can perfunctorily go through all the various elements of worship. The prayers, the music, the offering, the message, the appeal can all be characterized by a monotonous sameness. We need to be looking for and expecting that worship service that is strangely different - that holy hour when the Spirit is in complete control, that solemn and sobering moment when God moves in to inhabit the place where the saints are gathered, that electrifying slice of eternity when man's agenda is set aside in favor of God's agenda, that experience in worship that changes lives and sets the saints on high ground and revolutionizes the church.

The meeting of these saints was marked by a special obedience, a special oneness, and a special occasion.

The Meaning Of The Symbols

On the day of Pentecost the Holy Spirit was represented by two prominent instructive symbols. Luke declares, "And suddenly there came a sound from heaven as of a rushing, mighty wind, and it filled all the house where they were sitting. And there appeared unto them cloven tongues like as of fire, and it sat upon each of them. (Acts 2:2-3).

A Sudden Sound

The first symbol manifested was a sudden sound. The sound was like "a rushing, mighty wind." Once again we have the Greek word "pneuma" being translated "wind." The use of the word "wind" to symbolize the Spirit is certainly appropriate because both the wind and the Spirit are invisible, ethereal, mysterious, and yet very real. Moreover even as breath or wind is essential to the physical life of man, so is the Spirit of God necessary for the spiritual life of man.

This "sound from heaven as of a mighty, rushing wind" symbolized the advent of the Holy Spirit. Please notice that the Spirit did not come while these disciples were praying or beseeching or kneeling or seeking, but while they were "sitting." This simply signifies that the Holy Spirit was to be received as a gift. The Holy Spirit is not a reward for righteous deeds. He is a gift to those who believe on Jesus. Peter spoke of the gift of the Holy Spirit to believers in his sermon at Pentecost. In the Gentile Pentecost of Acts 10 the Bible declares, "And they of the circumcision which believed were astonished, as many as came with Peter, because that on the Gentiles also was poured out the gift of the Holy Ghost" (Acts 10:45).

Actually what we have in our text is not wind, but the sound of wind. Furthermore, the noise that was heard was like the frightening sound of a tumultuous tornado-like wind. I have heard people describe the awful sound of a tornado as being akin to the sound of a rumbling freight train. Perhaps the noise in the upper room was similar to the sound of an approaching train or a 767 airliner at take-off. With astounding suddenness, the noise filled the room. Though it sounded like wind, no one felt the effects of even the slightest zephyr. The roar was deafening, but the air was as calm as a Bethlehem night. The thunder of clamor was mysterious and inexplicable.

The origin of the sound, however, was obvious to all. The violent boom came from heaven. Perhaps the noise was simply God's way of getting the attention of the disciples in the upper room. Perhaps God used the sudden uproar to introduce the advent of the spirit. Perhaps the sound was the voice of the Lord Himself. In Revelation 1:15 the voice of the Lord is compared to "the sound of many waters." I have lived in the path of a hurricane, and I have also heard the sound of a "mighty, rushing wind." The two sounds are amazingly similar. The heavenly clamor was simply God's way of putting the disciples on notice that the third person of the Trinity was just about to enter the scene. What an amazing difference this holy, heavenly helper was to make in the lives of those first century believers.

The same Holy Spirit is available to the church today. But whether He is present or absent seems to make little difference to the average church member. The Spirit of God is so ignored in the modern church that it is almost hypocritical that we consider ourselves Trinitarian. Most of us are like the disciples of John encountered by Paul in Ephesus. Paul asked them, "Have you received the Holy Ghost since ye believed? They said unto Him, we have not so much as heard whether there be any Holy Ghost" (Acts 19:2). We have ignored the Holy Spirit in our ministries. We have slandered Him with our easy and lazy excuses. We have grieved Him with our casual and convenient Christianity to the extent that we stand helpless before a godless world in the crisis of the ages.

Many people are praying that the wind of God will begin to blow across our churches to bring another Pentecost. The truth of the matter is that we do not need another Pentecost anymore than we need another Bethlehem or another Calvary. We simply need to enjoy the Pentecost that God has promised to those who will allow their lives to be marked by a special obedience and oneness.

Today there are countless people who are insensitive to the entreaties and the overtures of Almighty God. Apparently they are waiting for God to get their attention through the sound of "many waters" or the sound of "a mighty, rushing wind." However, God does not always resort to dramatics to get attention. Elijah looked for God in the strong wind, the earthquake, and the fire, but the Lord was not to be found in these phenomena. Elijah finally heard from Jehovah in a still, small voice (see 1 Kings 19:11-12). Though God may communicate His will to us in some dramatic demonstration of the supernatural, He will more likely speak to our hearts through a still, small voice or through His Word. We must pray for God to give us a spiritual sensitivity to His word and His will.

A Spectacular Sight

The second symbol of the Holy Spirit in evidence on the day of Pentecost was manifested as a spectacular sight. The record states, "And there appeared unto them cloven tongues like as of fire, and it sat upon each of them" (Acts 2:3).

Think of all that fire can accomplish. Fire gives light; it illuminates. In an elementary school history class, we discovered that as a lad Abraham Lincoln would sit by the fireside at night reading books until the last flame flickered out. The fire provided light for the pages of his textbooks so that he could fill his mind with treasures of knowledge. The Holy Spirit provides the same kind of illumination. In fact, Jesus said, "I have yet many things to say unto you, but ye cannot bear them now. Howbeit when He, the Spirit of Truth, is come, He will guide you into all truth" (Jn. 16:12-13a).

Fire purifies. God's Holy Spirit is like a refiners fire that brings the impurities of our lives to the surface and exposes them and consumes them. The third person of the Trinity is the personality that convicts men of their sins—not just the obvious sins of the flesh, but also the hidden sins of the heart. The Holy Spirit turns the search light of God's holiness and the laser beam of heaven upon our simple hearts to purge, melt, and devour all that is unholy, earthly, or temporal.

Fire warms. When the apostle Paul was shipwrecked on the Island of Melita, the weather was cold and rainy. The natives of the island demonstrated their hospitality by kindling a fire to warm the victims of the shipwreck. The Holy Spirit sets the soul of the believer ablaze with joy, enthusiasm, and an unrestrained love for Jesus.

Many churches today are cold, dead, and formal. Only the Holy Spirit can ignite the fires of revival that will bring warmth and vitality to the modern day Laodiceas that are seemingly proliferating. Yet so often churches are cold and dying because the pulpit is not ablaze with a preacher who has a burning passion to preach the Gospel. It is not the preacher's job to fill the pews, but to fill the pulpit.

The church organist had been to the grocery store next door to the church and had come by the worship center to practice the music for Sunday's worship service. When the minister of music came into the auditorium, he noticed that she had put her grocery bag under the pulpit. He inquired, "Isn't the pulpit an unusual place to put your groceries while practicing the organ?"

"Oh no," the musician replied, "I've got four steaks and two pounds of ground beef that need to be kept cool and the pulpit is the coldest place in the church."

Preachers need to have their souls ignited with the fire of God's Holy Spirit. Jeremiah said, "But his word was in mine heart as a burning fire shut up in my bones..." (Jer. 20:9). Someone has said, "If the preacher gets on fire, the people will come and watch him burn." The Emmaus Road disciples encountered the risen Christ. They experienced a holy heartburn. They said, "Did not our hearts burn within us, while he talked with us by the way, and while he opened to us the Scriptures" (Lk. 24:32)? The pulpit and the pew need to have the Holy Spirit to kindle flames of sacred love and heavenly zeal in our hearts.

Fire spreads! The apostle James writes, "Behold, how great a matter a little fire kindleth!" (James 3:5b). The Chicago fire of

October 8, 1871, started when Mrs. O'Leary's cow kicked over a lantern. By the time this fire was extinguished, 17,450 buildings were destroyed, two hundred and fifty persons were killed, and the damage was estimated at $196 million. Similarly, the fire of the Holy Spirit can spread from one enthused, inspired believer to another until a sweeping revival results. In fact, that spark that was expressed as "cloven tongues of fire" upon the one hundred and twenty disciples on the day of Pentecost spread so rapidly that within two years the entire region had heard about the Lord Jesus Christ (see Acts 19:10-11).

Please note that the symbol was not only fire, but a tongue of fire. It is obvious that God wanted us to have a speaking, testifying, proclaiming church. Peter and John, filled with the Holy Spirit, said, "For we cannot but speak the things which we have seen and heard" (Acts 4:20). The spirit-filled believer will inevitably become the Master's messenger, heaven's herald, and Christ's courier.

Basically, in Biblical terminology, when the fire falls, God shows up. That is precisely what happened when Moses saw the bush being burned, yet not consumed. God spoke out of that bush and nearly scared Moses out of his sandals. When the fire fell in Elijah's day, the presence and the glory of God entered the scene to do what man could neither program, plan, manipulate, or perform through some illusionary hocus-pocus. On the day of Pentecost the "tongues of fire" indicated that God was on center stage to manifest His spirit in extraordinary measure.

Just remember that a sudden sound and a spectacular sight may indicate that God is about ready to show up. Before you get too thrilled, however, remember that when God shows up people are more comfortable on their faces on the floor than sitting in a pew. When God comes, there is fire and obvious conviction. Indifference is turned to mourning. Causal Christianity is exposed as an abomination to God. Half-hearted commitments are judged. Then Jesus is given His rightful place as Lord. The powerful Holy Spirit begins to produce life and spontaneity and reality.

The Ministry Of The Spirit

Please notice that following the sudden sound and the spectacular sight that "they were all filled with the Holy Ghost." This "filling of the Holy Spirit" was an often-repeated experience among those disciples of the first century. For example, in Acts 4:8 we read that "Peter was filled with the Holy Ghost." Once again, in Acts 4:31, "they were all filled with the Holy Ghost." When the apostles needed some men to assist them in the work of the ministry, the church selected seven men who were "full of the Holy Ghost"(Acts 6:3). When Ananias visited Saul of Tarsus after his conversion, he said, "Brother Saul, the Lord, even Jesus... hath sent me, that thou mightiest receive thy sight, and be filled with the Holy Ghost"(Acts 9:17) In one of the most beautiful biographical sketches in all of the Bible, the apostle Luke describes Barnabas as a "good man and full of the Holy Ghost and of faith" (Acts 11:24). In Acts 13:9 the Bible declares that Paul was "full of the Holy Ghost." Then Luke relates in Acts 13:52 that "...the disciples were filled with joy, and with the Holy Ghost."

However, this experience of being filled with the Holy Spirit was not reserved just for the early church. Neither is this infilling allocated only to the pastor, the evangelist, or to some spiritually elite group. Every Christian can have this happy, holy, heart-warming experience. In fact, being filled with the Spirit is not just a promise to enjoy; it is a command to obey. In Ephesians 5:17-18 the apostle Paul declares, "Wherefore be ye not unwise but understanding what the will of the Lord is and be not drunk with wine, wherein is excess; but be filled with the Spirit."

Indeed, the Holy Spirit has many operations to perform in the course of His ministry. For example, the Holy Spirit baptizes; the Holy Spirit indwells; the Holy Spirit seals; the Holy Spirit gives gifts; the Holy Spirit produces fruit; and the Holy Spirit anoints. Volumes have been written about the person and the work of the Holy Spirit.

For our purposes, however, we are going to limit our focus to the infilling of the Holy Spirit. What does it mean to be filled with the Holy Spirit? To be filled with the Spirit of God is to be dominated, controlled, led, and governed by the Holy Spirit. Every child of God needs this divine infilling. The nursery worker in the extended session during the worship hour may very well need this heavenly infilling just as surely as the man who stands behind the pulpit to deliver the sermon.

The notable preacher and teacher, Dr. Howard Hendricks, once told the story of a speaking engagement he had in California a number of years ago. He had been invited to speak to thousands of young people at Anaheim Stadium, the home of the California Angels baseball team. As he sat on the platform waiting for the opportunity to speak, he said, "What a great opportunity and responsibility. I desperately need the infilling and the anointing of the Holy Spirit for this remarkable occasion."

Later Dr. Hendricks said, "The Spirit of God flooded my soul and endued me with power as I spoke. The next day I flew back home, basking in the afterglow of that experience. My wife met me at the airport and began to tell me the many things that were awaiting my attention when I got home. The children needed me. The dog needed me. There were chores to be done. The lawn needed my attention.

"Then she said, 'Howard, the sewage system is backed up. The bathroom facilities are not working and you need to do something about it.'"

Immediately after arriving home Dr. Hendricks exchanged his three-piece suit for a rather ragged pair of trousers. He turned off all of the faucets and started the process of digging a hole in the yard in order to fix the drain. As he began to dig he thought, "This is not exactly what I had viewed as the job of an evangelist." As he dug that hole he became weary with the toilsome task. He dug four feet down into the earth. He was perspiring. He was weary. He was irritated that he, who had just the night before spoken to thousands of young people in the splendor of Anaheim Stadium, was four feet beneath the ground in an effort to fix the sewage line.

Just then his four-year-old son used the bathroom and turned on everything. Suddenly the contents of the clogged sewage line emerged like a great geyser and the great Bible teacher was sprayed with it all. He said, "In that moment I needed the infilling and the anointing of the Holy Spirit to produce His fruit in my life. In fact, I needed more of the Holy Spirit in that unpleasant, irritating, moment that I needed when I stood up before the splendor of that great crowd at Anaheim Stadium the night before."

The infilling of the Holy Spirit is not restricted to the preacher who stands in the pulpit to proclaim the unsearchable riches of Christ. Indeed, it is needed in that strategic moment, but it must also work in the mundane, routine experiences of daily living. The mother needs to be filled with the Holy Spirit as she seeks to meet the demands of her little ones who are constantly pulling at her apron strings. The businessman needs to be filled with the Holy Spirit when he concludes his negotiation on that important business deal. The high school baseball player needs to be filled with the Holy Spirit when he strikes out with the bases loaded. The teenage girl needs to be filled with the Holy Spirit when she finds out that she was not selected to be on the cheerleading squad.

Revival becomes a reality when God's people demonstrate in every circumstance of life that they are dominated and controlled by the Spirit of God. Revival becomes a reality when believers consistently walk not after the flesh, but after the Spirit. Revival is a reality when the children of God are led by the Spirit of God to boldly share their faith to a lost and dying world. Revival becomes a reality when spirit-filled saints have as their primary purpose in life the glorification of Jesus Christ. When these things happen, you will know that the wind and the fire of heaven have come down to earth.

"Abandon hope, all ye who enter here!"

Inscription over the gates of hell in Dante's Inferno

"It would be dreadful to suffer this fierceness and wrath of Almighty God for one moment: but you must suffer it for all eternity."

Jonathan Edwards - Sinners in the Hands of an Angry God

"Some will not be redeemed. There is no doctrine which I would more willingly remove from Christianity than this (the doctrine of hell) if it lay in my power."

C. S. Lewis - The Problem of Pain [20]

The Torment Of Tophet
Isaiah 30:33

"For Tophet is ordained of old; yea, for the king it is prepared; he hath made it deep and large: the pile thereof is fire and much wood; the breath of the lord, like a stream of brimstone, doth kindle it." Isaiah 30:33

During the decade of the 1970's I had the privilege of serving as the pastor of the First Baptist Church of Camden, South Carolina. On numerous occasions while living in this beautiful and historic town, I heard some venerable citizen recount the story of the Cleveland School fire that occurred on May 17, 1923. This terrible, tragic fire burned up a schoolhouse and brought a sudden death to 76 young people whose lives had brimmed with enthusiasm.

Frantic parents and horror stricken neighbors looked at the blazing inferno in a delirium of mind shattering helplessness. Above the sound of the crackling flames and the falling timbers, the onlookers could hear the cries of those who begged for release from the prison house of torturous flames. The shrieking cry of burning children from this death trap of torment was so seared into the minds of those who witnessed that holocaust that its haunting effect continues to the present day.

In the round of ministerial duties, I have occasionally visited burn victims in hospital rooms and observed the agony, the disfigurement, even the characteristic stench that often permeates the rooms of such patients. Secondary infections: gangrene, nephritis, pneumonia, erysipelas, intestinal disturbances, vomiting, and convulsions often complicate serious burns. Excruciating pain and serious medical complications are often the result of being the victim of a blazing inferno.

Fire can be man's best friend or his worst enemy. A flame of fire can provide light for the darkness, warmth for the cold, and many other blessings. However, the suffering resulting from being burned by fire can be indescribably tormenting. In the Bible "Tophet" is a place of fire, a place of torment, and a preview of hell, God's penitentiary for the damned.

The Picture Of This Place

Tophet was located "in the valley of the sun of Hinnom" (Jer. 7:31). This valley is situated outside the city of Jerusalem "by the entry of the east gate" (Jer. 19:2). The false God Moloch was worshiped in this place (Jer. 32:35). Although Hebrew law strictly prohibited the worship of Moloch (Lev. 18:21), Solomon built an altar to this detestable deity at Tophet in the valley of the sun of

Hinnom. First, the ancient Canaanites worshiped Moloch by offering their children as burnt offerings to appease the wrath of this pagan deity. Then the apostate Israelites led by King Ahaz and King Manasseh took up this practice until Tophet became a place of abomination and torment (2 Kings 16:1-3 and 2 Kings 21:1-6). The fiendish custom of offering infants as a sacrifice to the god of fire seems to have been kept up in Tophet for a considerable period of time. This despicable place therefore became known for its fire, its agony, its torment, and its crying, suffering, dying children.

When King Josiah came on the scene, he sought to institute a reformation of righteousness. He tore down the pagan altars and rendered Tophet ceremonially unclean by cutting down the groves and filling the whole area with human bones (2 Kings 23:14). Tophet became the cesspool of the city, the depository of its sewerage and solid filth. The repugnant place also became the receptacle for all executed malefactors and unclaimed bodies: and these unclean corpses were left to burn or undergo decomposition in this valley of misery and squalor. Tophet was a foul smelling place of pollution and corruption.

The word "Tophet" is extremely interesting and has at least three possible derivations. For example, many scholars believe that the word is derived from the Hebrew "toph" which means "drum." This idea originates from the drums or the tabrets that were beaten upon to drown out the cries of the children who were made to pass through the fire of Moloch. There are others who contend that "Tophet" roots back to the word "tuth" meaning to "to spit." This concept conveys the idea that Tophet was a place to be spat upon, a place of infamy and abomination. Absalom's tomb in the Valley of Kedron has been regarded for many years as a place to be spat upon. This tomb is regarded as a place of abomination because Absalom rebelled against his father and tried to usurp his father's throne. Therefore, like the tomb of Absalom, Tophet was considered to be a place of disgrace and shame. Other scholars have concluded that Tophet has its origin in the word "tophteh" which means "contempt" and signifies the place where dead bodies are cremated or burned. In any event we can be sure that Tophet was a place to be abhorred and a place to be viewed with horror.

Although Tophet is used by Isaiah to describe the destiny of Assyria, the archenemy of Israel, we can be sure that it is also prophetically portrayed as a type or a figure of hell, the place of eternal torment. In the New Testament "hell" is a translation of the Greek word "geena" which is actually a transliteration of the Hebrew "Hehinnon" which means "the Valley of Hinnom: which was the location of Tophet. So, there is a definite connection between "tophet" in the Old Testament and "hell" in the New Testament. Both words actually refer to a place, which in Jewish thought symbolized eternal punishment – a place where continual fires burned, where rubbish befouled the landscape, and a place infested with many worms.

Jesus said that it would be far better to have radical surgery and amputate a hand or foot or pluck out an eye than "to be cast into hell, into the fire that shall never be quenched: where their worm dieth not, and the fire is not quenched" (Mark 9:45-46).

The Provision Of This Place

The text indicates that "Tophet is ordained of old…" God's justice demands that a means of punishment be established for those who rebel against Him. Assyria, having set themselves against God was destined for destruction. The king would be the greatest victim of this retribution. God ordained it to be so. Similarly, God prepared hell for the devil and his fallen angels, but those whose names are not written in the Lamb's Book of Life will also face the same retribution as Satan and his dominion of demons. Jewish tradition holds to the view that hell was made by God on the second day of creation. The Talmud seems to affirm the view of hell being created before the world was formed.

In our day a modern, sophisticated society dominated by a doctrine of tolerance wants to discount the idea of hell. Many would say, "If there is a God, He would certainly be a benevolent God; and if He were a benevolent God, He would be a God of love; and if He were a God of love. He would not create a race of people and then punish a great host of them in a place like hell."

The preceding view may express the philosophy of our present day society, but God's book says, "Evil men understand not judgment: but they that seek the Lord understand all things" (Prov. 28:5). God is omniscient; and if in His wisdom He determined to prepare a place for the righteous. He surely had to prepare a place for the unrighteous and unbelieving. For God to do otherwise would alter His character and remove the equilibrium from His sovereignty. A gracious, loving God who is not just is like a sentimental grandfather. A just, powerful God who is not loving and gracious is like an insensitive baronial landlord. However, the God whose character includes mercy and justice, love and power, holiness and wisdom is the God worthy of our worship and devotion.

The provision of Tophet gives us a picture of God that is complete and comprehensive. He has provided for the just and the unjust, the redeemed and the unredeemed, the saved and the lost. There is favor for the saint and fire for the sinner. There is glory for the believer and gloom for the unbeliever. There is heaven for the child of God and hell for the child of the devil. God has provided for us the torment of Tophet and the blessedness of Beulah land. The provisions of both are essential in order for Him to maintain His character of holiness.

The Purpose Of This Place

Isaiah tells us that Tophet was prepared for "the king." The immediate reference is to the king of Assyria whose end was sure to come according to the Word of God. A greater prophetic implication is doubtlessly to Satan, the ruler of this world of darkness (Jn. 14:30 and Jn. 16:11). Satan is referred to as "the prince of this world." The Greek word for "prince" is "archon" which means "ruler" or "king." Indeed, Jesus declared that "the everlasting fire [of hell was] prepared for the devil and his angels" (Matt. 25:41). Satan is the diabolical fiend who led an army of angels to sin in rebellion against God. He was the sinister serpent who caused Adam and Eve to commit the sin that resulted in their expulsion from Eden's paradise. He even launched a vicious attack upon the Son of God in an effort to blemish His character and thwart His mission. He is the master of deceit and the architect of every dirty, depraved, devilish, death-dealing sin in the whole world.

None of us can conceive of the demented mind and dreadful wickedness of Satan. There was a time, when as an archangel in heaven, he had perfect light and lived in the radiance of God's righteousness and the glow of His glory. Yet, through pride and ambition, he set out to usurp God's place of preeminence in the universe. Lucifer's self-willed strategy to be God's rival and wrest this universe from the control of its Maker resulted in his being forced out of heaven and cast down to the earth and ultimately to hell (Is. 14:12-15).

The existence of Satan makes hell an absolute necessity. There are those who declare that they do not believe in hell. Even human rationale should be able to conclude that it is more reasonable and more benevolent for God to cast the devil into hell than to allow him to continue to walk about as a roaring lion who devours his prey. For thousands of years Satan has been vehemently opposed to God, to Christ, to the church, and has endeavored to ruin everything God has created. Therefore, the devil is regarded by the Heavenly Father to be "public enemy number one" and God has appropriately made reservations for him in this eternal prison house of despair called hell. Furthermore, Satan will not be the lord of hell. He will not be the warden in this penitentiary of the doomed. In fact, he will have the hot spot on God's rotisserie in this place designed not for his presidency, but for his punishment.

The Proportions Of This Place

Isaiah identifies Tophet as a place that has been made "deep and large." Actually, the Valley of Hinnom where Tophet is located begins on the west side of Jerusalem at the Jaffa gate and continues southward until it bends east along the southern limits of the city. The Valley of Hinnom joins the Kedron Valley near the southeastern corner of Jerusalem near the dung gate. The valley of Hinnom is a deep ravine with steep, rocky sides. The adjectives used to describe the proportions of Tophet seem to confirm that this place is symbolic of hell. Jesus preached, "Enter ye in at the strait gate: for wide is the gate, and broad is the way, that leadeth to destruction, and many there be which go in thereat" (Matt. 7:13).

Several years ago my wife and I traveled to Boston for a vacation. One afternoon we took a tour of the city. When we got to some of the narrow, cobblestone streets near Beacon Street, the tour guide said, "Many years ago it was decided that if two pregnant cows could meet and successfully pass by each other on these streets, they would be designated as two-way streets." Those "two-way" cobblestone streets were far too narrow for two lanes of automobile traffic. They were not smooth and offered rough, uncomfortable rides. Some of those streets had sharp curves and uphill and downhill places. Furthermore, those alleyways were very infrequently traveled. On the contrary, the super highways of our present day offer smooth travel, beautiful scenery, and easy access. Consequently, many people avail themselves of the smooth sailing afforded by the six-to-ten-lane ribbons of asphalt that stretch from city to city across the continent. So it is with the broad road that leads to destruction. "Many there be which go in thereat."

We have already concluded that the devil will be the chief resident in the Tophet of torment. The angels that identified with Satan in his revolt against God will also be numbered among the citizens of this city of flaming fire. In Jude 6 we are told: "And the angels which kept not their first estate, but left their own habitation, he hath delivered in everlasting chains under darkness unto the judgment of the great day."

The Bible also speaks of demons, unclean spirits, and devils all around us in the world today. The Gadarene demoniac was possessed by a legion of devils. The evil spirits that were operating in this poor demented man had warped his mind and put it in his heart to wear no clothes, mutilate his body, and live among the tombstones of a graveyard. The demons had given him a super human strength to break the chains that men would dare to use to bind him.

When Jesus confronted this disturbed, distraught man, the demons urged Him to ask, "What have I to do with thee, Jesus, thou son of the most high God? I adjure thee by God, that thou torment me not" (Mark 5:7). The evil spirits requested to be cast into a herd of swine feeding nearby. They obviously knew their ultimate habitation and preferred to occupy swine to the torment that was inevitable. In fact, in Matthew 8:29, we are informed that these demons cried out to Jesus, " What have we to do with thee, Jesus, thou Son of God? Art thou come hither to torment us before the time?" This legion of devils somehow knew that their fate was sealed and hell was their destiny. They did not want Jesus to begin their punishment "before the time."

Several years ago I had a woman from Corpus Christi, Texas to visit me in my church study. She professed to be a witch and had been greatly involved in the occult. She had trafficked in drugs and sexual perversions of the most bizarre descriptions. I listened in horror as she unveiled the ways in which the powers of darkness had captured and nearly destroyed her life. The demons that possessed the Gadarene demoniac and the evil spirits that had taken control of this young woman from Texas will be numbered among the hideous, horrible hosts of hell. These evil, unclean spirits make hell a necessity. Their incarceration in this pit of punishment is a part of God's design.

In the book of Revelation we are informed that the beast and the false prophet will also be cast into hell. The apostle John declares in Revelation 19:20: "And the beast was taken, and with him the false prophet that wrought miracles before him, with which he deceived them that had received the mark of the beast, and them that worshiped his image. These both were cast alive into a lake of fire burning with brimstone."

Also in Revelation the apostle declares that the wicked of all ages one day will dwell in hell: "But the fearful and unbelieving, and the abominable, and murderers, and whoremongers, and sorcerers, and idolaters, and all liars, shall have their part in the lake which burneth with fire and brimstone; which is the second death"(Rev. 21:8). Hell is going to be a place of vile association. Have you ever heard anyone say, "Well, if I go to hell, I will have plenty of company"? Indeed, there will be a numberless host in hell. Every vile, wicked, perverted, lascivious person who has ever lived will be there.

Though hell will be thronged with people, it will be a place of total isolation. Those who are sentenced to this burning caldron will never see another person. Hell is a place of dismal darkness. The fires of hell are so designed by God that although they produce heat, they do not produce light. Jesus described hell as a place of unnatural darkness and agony. He indicated that the unprofit-able servant would be cast "into outer darkness where there shall be weeping and gnashing of teeth" (Matt. 25:30). Jude portrays the destiny of the unsaved as those "...to whom is reserved the blackness of darkness forever" (Jude 13). These wicked and unre-pentant inhabitants of hell will spend eternity alone in a fiery pit of darkness.

Notice the ones who lead the list of those destined for doom. The first ones on the list in Revelation 21:8 are "the fearful and unbelieving." The person who does not believe in Jesus Christ and does not have the courage to confess Jesus Christ is number one on the list of the damned. Consider what the Bible says about the sin of unbelief. "He that believeth on him is not condemned; but he that believeth not is condemned already, because he hath not believed in the name of the only begotten Son of God" (Jn. 3:18). So it is easy to go to hell. Just relax; put it in neutral; take the course of least resistance. Do nothing about Jesus, and you will end up in an eternal Tophet.

Furthermore, hell will have to be a large and spacious place because it will be inhabited by hypocrites. In the Sermon on the Mount, Jesus said, "Not everyone that saith unto me. Lord, Lord, shall enter into the kingdom of heaven; but he that doth the will of my Father which is in heaven. Many will say to me in that day, Lord, Lord, have we not prophesied in thy name? And in thy name have cast out devils? And in thy name done many wonderful works? And then will I profess unto them, I never knew you: depart from me, ye that work iniquity" (Matt. 7:21-23).

Perhaps the chief hypocrite in hell will be Judas Iscariot. Judas was one of the disciples of Christ and a man highly respected by his peers. He was chosen to be the treasurer of the group, and the other eleven disciples never doubted his integrity. Judas no doubt fulfilled a ministry, served others, and heralded the truth about Jesus, but was never converted. He never trusted Christ for his salvation. In John 6:64, Jesus said, "But there are some of you that believe not." Then we read, "But Jesus knew from the beginning who they were that believed not, and who should betray him."

Then in verses 70-71 we read, "Jesus answered them, have not I chosen you twelve, and one of you is a devil? He spake of Judas Iscariot, the son of Simon: for he it was that should betray him being one of the twelve." Dr. Adrian Rogers stated, "In betraying Jesus Judas Iscariot kissed the door of heaven and went to hell as the chief of all hypocrites."

The Bible tells us that "whosoever was not found written in the Book of Life was cast into the lake of fire" (Rev. 20:15). So, Tophet, which is given in the Bible as a type of hell, is described as "deep and large." Similarly, the proportions of hell will be great because "many there be which go in thereat" (Matt. 7:13).

The Pyre Of This Place

"Pyre" is a word that means "a combustible heat for burning a dead body" or "a pile of material to be burned." In the eternal Tophet of God's retribution against the unredeemed, Isaiah describes the pyre thusly: "The pile thereof is fire and much wood; the breath of the Lord, like a stream of brimstone, doth kindle it" (Is. 30:33c).

Occasionally the question is asked, "Do you believe what the Bible teaches about hell to be figurative or to be literal?" I have decided to believe it the way God wrote it and preach it literally. If, in heaven, I discover I was wrong, I would prefer to have God say, "You took my Word too seriously," than to have Him say, "Preacher, you should never have diluted and compromised my Holy Word." I prefer to take sides with the old-fashioned evangelist who declared, "If God didn't mean what He said, why didn't He say what He meant?"

Now there are those who believe that hell is in the heart of the earth. These learned men state that Tophet's location down in the Valley of Hinnom signifies that hell is down in the bowels of the earth. Many books addressing the subject of geology talk about the geothermal energy within the earth's crust. Many believe that there is evidence to show that these geothermal reservoirs underneath the surface of the earth are rapidly growing in capacity and intensity. In fact, in geology there is a scale known as a geothermal gradient. This gradient specifies that as a general rule there is an increase in the temperature of the earth from its surface down to its core. The increase is estimated to be one degree Fahrenheit per sixty feet. Essentially the earth's interior is extremely hot. Only thirty miles down where volcanic lava is formed, the temperature is thought to be about twenty-two hundred degrees Fahrenheit. At the center of the earth some speculate that the temperature could be as high as seventy-two hundred degrees Fahrenheit, which would approach the temperature that exists on the surface of the sun.

The Scripture gives some credence to the belief that hell is under the earth or in the very core of the earth. In Philippians 2:10-11, we are told that the day is coming when Jesus will be acknowledged as Lord by those in heaven, those in earth, and those under the earth. Unfortunately, this recognition and worship will take place after the day of grace has passed. However, in that day all of creation will see Jesus for who He is. Even those "under the earth" will bow the knee and "confess that Jesus Christ is Lord."

When the rich man of Luke 16 died and went to hell, the Bible says that he lifted up his eyes and saw Abraham afar off. The fact that he lifted up his eyes indicates that he was down and that

Abraham was up. Could it be that hell is a literal, physical place down in the heart of the earth?

In Revelation 9:1-3, Satan is described as a star that fell from heaven to the earth. The Word declares: "...and to him was given the key to the bottomless pit. And he opened the bottomless pit; and there arose a smoke out of the pit, as the smoke of a great furnace; and the sun and the air were darkened by reason of the smoke of the pit. And there came out of the smoke locusts upon the earth: and unto them was given power, as the scorpions of the earth have power."

There are those who contend that the bottomless pit is hell and that Satan will come down to earth one day to open the bottomless pit. When this horror chamber is opened, the smoke and fire of hell itself will leap out; and a host of hideous, repugnant, demonic creatures will be unleashed on the human family. These evil spirits will not kill or destroy, but they will create such havoc and misery that men will seek death. The speculation is, however, that hell is below us, down in the center of the earth.

If you are not prepared to accept the bowels of the earth as the location of hell, perhaps you will steadfastly agree that God is able to use His own ingenious methods of pyrotechnics to fan the flames of Tophet. Our text informs us that "the breath of the Lord, like a stream of brimstone, doth kindle it." The God who breathed the world into existence and breathed into man's nostrils the breath of life will blow like a bellows upon the flames of hell to produce a remarkable intensive heat that will burn but not consume.

Many times Boy Scouts have started fires with sticks or flint rocks. At first there is smoke, then sparks, and at last, with the help of a lot of hot air blown from the lungs of anxious campers, a genuine flame of fire. Oxygen is essential to fire. Therefore, God, who would prefer to breathe life into the soul of man, with tears in his eyes breathes that which kindles the flame of Tophet. It is a scorching, searing flame that knows no end to the intensive agony that it produces. In this life there are limitations that restrict the degree to which pain can afflict us. In the present day intense pain can be terminated by the loss of consciousness or by death. In hell neither of those merciful experiences will bring one moment's reprieve to the torment of that dreadful, everlasting fire.

Dr. Stan Coffey, pastor of the San Jacinto Baptist Church (The Church at Quail Creek) in Amarillo, Texas, tells the story about a young man from Cleveland, Ohio, who worked in a chemical factory. In this particular factory chemists discovered a chemical that had a strange and violent reaction when mixed with water. The chemical seemed to have the ability to dissolve water. A few drops of this chemical in an ounce of water would cause the water to be reduced to a puff of smoke.

This young man decided that he would use this newly discovered chemical to have some fun with his friends. He stole a vial of this powerful liquid from the laboratory. Several days later when he had several houseguests visiting his home, he decided that he would demonstrate the amazing properties of this volatile chemical. The friends gathered in a circle and he put a drop of the chemical in a cup of water. The water disintegrated in a miniature mushroom cloud of smoke.

Then he thought he would really captivate the attention of his guests with a spectacular demonstration. He ran his bathtub full of water. He had a whole vial of that chemical in his hand. As he marched over toward this tub, he tripped and that whole vial of fluid spilled out into that tub of water. As his equilibrium gave way, he fell in the bathtub and the entire upper part of his body was submerged in the water. The reaction of that chemical upon his skin began to burn. The man cried out in agony, "I'm on fire! Somebody do something! I'm on fire!"

In torment the man clutched at his clothes and began to tear away his shirt from his body. Once again he cried, "Please help me! I'm on fire!"

They could not help him. There was nothing they could do. The paramedics came and took him to the emergency room of the hospital. After they had taken his clothes from his body, the nurse took a damp sponge and, as she would have customarily done for a burn victim, began to gently apply that sponge to his burning brow. But when the moisture touched his skin, once again the chemical would react and flames would literally leap from that young man's body, and he would cry out, "I am in hell! I am on fire! I am in hell! I am on fire! Somebody help me! I am in hell! I am on fire!"

The doctor came and literally removed the outer layer of skin from the body of that young man, but even then if there was any contact with moisture, flames would leap from the pores of his skin and he would cry out, "I'm on fire! I'm in hell! I'm on fire!" It was not long, however, until death mercifully came and brought an end to his misery.

I want you to remember that Jesus said that there is a place where "the fire is never quenched and where the worm dieth not" (Mark

9:44, 46, 48). That is the place where the screams of those who are there for all eternity are never quieted and their torment never ends.

Author's Notes

1. Paul Richardson, "God the Creator – The Creator Song," website: http://www.allaboutcreation.org/god-the-creator.htm

2. The Keswick Week, 1951, p. 128 - Sermon by Donald Grey Barnhouse on "The Breath of God." Published by Marshall, Morgan & Scott, LTD, London.

3. Ibid, p. 128.

4. John F. MacArthur, The Creation of Man, sermon preached at Grace Community Church in Panorama City, California, 1999.

5. Seneca, Lucius Annaeus, On the Shortness of Life, First Century A.D.

6. Spurgeon, Charles Haddon, The Treasury of the Bible - Volume 3, Grand Rapids, Michigan: Zondervan Publishing House, 1968), 273.

7. Meyer, F. B., Gospel of John, (Fort Washington, PA, Christian Literature Crusade, 1992)

8. Criswell, W. A. Old Time Religion, preached multiple times during Criswell's ministry at First Baptist Church in Dallas, Texas.

9. Taylor, Jack R. Victory Over the Devil, (Nashville: Broadman Press, 1973).

10. "Church Moved By The Hand of God" brochure produced by the Providence Methodist Church, Swan Quarter, N. C.

11. Blackaby, Henry T., Experiencing the Spirit: The Power of Pentecost Every Day, Multnomah Press, United States, 2009.

12. Blanchard, John, Gathered Gold: A Treasury of Quotations for Christians, (Darlington, UK, Evangelical Press, 2006), 187.

13. Ibid, *187*.

14. *Ignatius,* The Lord of the Sabbath, *website: http://www.sound-doctrine.net/Nick/Lord_Sabbath.htm.*

15. *Lee, Robert G.,* The Bible and Prayer, *(Nashville, Convention Press,1950), 2.*

16. *Vines, Jerry,* A Baptist and His Bible, *preached during the Southern Baptist Convention in St. Louis, Missouri, in 1987.*

17. *Easum, Bill,* Signs of a Spiritually-Dead Church, *(Wellington, New Zealand, Jubilee Resources International, Inc.) website: http://www.jubilee.org.nz/.*

18. *J. B. Lawrence,* The Holy Spirit in Missions *(Atlanta: Home Mission Board, Southern Baptist Convention, 1947), 87.*

19. *Doug Knapp, Robert O'Brien, Evelyn Knapp,* Thunder in the Valley *(Nashville, B & H Publishing Group, 1986), 64.*

20. *C.S. Lewis,* The Problem of Pain, *(HarperOne, February 6, 2001)*

CPSIA information can be obtained at www.ICGtesting.com
Printed in the USA
LVOW012324220812

295548LV00001B/7/P